UNDERSTANDING
STRESS

UNDERSTANDING STRESS

Dilys Hartland

CAXTON REFERENCE

© 2000 Caxton Editions

This edition published 2000 by Caxton Editions,
20 Bloomsbury Street, London, WC1B 3QA.

Caxton Editions is an imprint of the Caxton Publishing Group.

Printed and bound in India .

CONTENTS

PART 2: HEALING FROM WITHIN

PART 3: COPING FROM THE OUTSIDE

PART 1
UNDERSTANDING

WHAT IS STRESS?

The stress response

Nature has equipped all animals with a means of coping with stress. There is a 'stress response' programmed into our bodies – a surge of adrenaline, which is the stress hormone that presses the red button for 'fight or flight' – that gives us a rush of energy to deal with the emergency facing us. Dry mouth, pounding heart, the urge to urinate (and so make the body lighter for running), rapid breathing (needed to take in more oxygen in fleeing from an attacker) - all these physical responses to stress are ways in which our bodies automatically prepare us to deal with situations in our external environment which may be dangerous for us.

Stress is not new; it has always been a part of our life on this planet. But in the animal world – and the world we used to inhabit – stress generally refers to real, physical emergencies – a fox in the hen house, or the response of a fox hearing the cry of hounds. Enemies approaching; the castle surrounded.

The trouble is, we are not meant to maintain that heightened state of alertness for long. We are meant to evaluate that outside cause of stress (the stressor), deal with it, and calm down again.

Scientists have described the response to stress as occurring in three phases:

1. Alarm *('Oh my God! What's going on?')*. This is when the physical stress response takes over to prepare the body for immediate action.

2. Adaptation *('I'm just going to have to cope with this')*. The body hunkers down for a prolonged period of living with stress, such as may happen after a bereavement. Think of people in the Blitz, living under sustained bombardment. The secretion of further hormones increases blood sugar levels and the blood pressure rises. If this siege goes on for too long, the body starts to suffer tiredness, irritability, and a loss of concentration.

3. Exhaustion. The body's resources, worn out with over-long exposure to a source of stress, begin to deplete.

What do we mean by stress?
For many of us, stress is defined not as that immediate moment of danger or risk demanding a cool head and a calm response (such as may be felt by a soldier on active duty, or a mountain climber, or someone playing a potentially dangerous sport) but in terms of that period of adaptation described above.

Stress is day after day of dealing with the same apparently unsolvable problems, day after day of facing the same unrewarding situations.

Stress is when there seems to be no room in our lives for all the various bits of us. Stress is when we feel we're losing the plot.

The world around us in the twenty-first century holds numerous potential sources of stress – noise, pollution, traffic, financial pressures, a fiercely competitive working environment – and few of us can escape them. I'd imagine that even living on a desert island might have its own particular set of pressures – loneliness, perhaps, or a lack of stimulation.

We should always remember, however, that stress also has its positive, beneficial aspects. It exists for a purpose (to help us survive) and, properly managed, helps spur us to perform to the best of our ability. The performer waiting in the wings to go on stage is under stress: but without that fear response, he or she wouldn't have 'edge', that crucial adrenaline buzz that creates a great performance. A football team competing in a key match is under stress, and they need to be – the pounding hearts, the acute awareness of self that stress brings, all these contribute to the keenness of their playing. A sportsman not feeling stressed is likely to be a dull performer who doesn't much care whether he wins or loses, whereas stress makes winning vital.

We could all write a list of the things in life that cause us to feel stressed. These can range from the apparently trivial – rush-hour traffic, crowded public transport, supermarket queues – to the more serious: confrontations at work or in the home, health worries, family problems. (I say 'apparently' trivial because we should take seriously anything that diminishes the quality of our lives. When stress makes our lives less easy to live than they should be, we need to investigate why.)

If you have a piece of paper handy, do it now. Write down five things in your life that cause you stress. We'll come back to that list later.

Tired all the time

It is widely acknowledged that many illnesses on the increase in modern society are stress-related. These include heart disease, asthma, diabetes, ulcers, digestive disorders and skin complaints. Being under long-term stress does not necessarily cause eczema or diabetes, but if you have the underlying tendency towards that condition, stress can bring about its full-blown onset.

It has been estimated that over 80 per cent of people who walk into a doctor's surgery do so with a stress-related complaint.

Sometimes the symptoms of illness are obvious, but often people go to the doctor saying just that they're 'tired all the time'. This is such a common complaint that doctors have shorthand in their notes for it: TATT. This fatigue is the end result of the 'adaptation' phase of living with stress: the body descends into a chronic state of exhaustion; there may be no other physical symptom except just 'not feeling well'.

Let's simplify things by looking at stress in two ways: stress that arises from things that happen to us in our lives – a response to a life event; and stress that just seems to be, to come unprompted from within ourselves, so that we can feel stress even without any particular event to hang it on to.

Life events

Two Americans, Holmes and Rahe, developed a list
of 'life events' they deemed as stressful, and
accorded a weighting to each event. If you score
100–199 your crisis is supposedly 'mild', whereas a
score of 300 indicates a major life crisis.

Bereavement	100
Divorce	73
Relationship breakdown	65
Imprisonment	63
Death of a close relative or friend	63
Personal injury or illness	53
Marriage/engagement/cohabitation	50
Loss of job	47
Reconcilation in a married relationship	45
Retirement	45
Illness in the family	44
Pregnancy	44
Sexual problems	39
Birth of a child	39
Changes or adjustments at work	39
Changes in financial status	38
New job	36
Financial worries e.g. over-extended mortgage, debt	31
Son or daughter leaving home	29
Outstanding personal achievement	28
Starting or finishing at school or any other type of educational course	26

Moving house	20
Changes in your social life	19
Going on holiday	16
Christmas	12

The weighting given to these events is highly subjective, however, and I wouldn't take your 'score' too seriously. (Nobody would describe bereavement as a mild crisis). For instance, someone with financial worries may feel that their whole life has been taken over by that anxiety – if you feel that you are having a major life crisis, then you are!

It's also the case that the more of these events you are dealing with at any particular time, the more stress you are under. If, for example, someone whose relationship (married or otherwise) has recently ended is also facing financial pressures and worries and the task of moving house, that person will be under enormous strain. It's a useful checklist for bosses to bear in mind when looking after their staff: if you know that people working for you are undergoing any one (or more) of the above, be aware that their stress levels are likely to be high.

What's curious about this list is how many of these events are joyful ones (pregnancy or the birth of a child, for instance) – yet even these are listed as sources of stress. The reason lies in the fact that all of them represent change, and to Holmes and Rahe who devised the list all change is stressful. We're creatures of habit and routine. We seem programmed to let our lives toddle along in the same old way: up at a certain hour, off to work by the same train, home at the same time, television on Mondays, exercise class on Tuesdays, the supermarket on Fridays and the garden at the weekend. The truth is, we like our routines and they give us stability. Anything that interrupts that stability may cause us stress. Change represents the unknown.

In the case of an 'outstanding personal achievement', stress may come from the feeling that we've reached the top in a career or an endeavour, and that there is nothing left to do or to achieve. Maybe, even, having been promoted so far, we may now even be on the way out, ripe for redundancy so that younger people can take over. Does the Oscar winner feel 'that's it', there's nothing to try for any more? That conqueror of ancient times, Alexander the Great, is reported to have wept 'There are no more worlds to conquer' when he achieved mastery of the then-known world. With nothing left to achieve, he died in 323 BC at the age of thirty-three.

Look again at pregnancy as a source of stress. The baby may be completely wanted and the birth eagerly awaited, but the mother-to-be may also be anxious about the future. How will she cope? What if she makes mistakes? If she is going to be a working mother, the stresses will be greater – will her childcare arrangements be safe and happy for the child? Will the child suffer if she goes back to work, and how will the mother herself suffer if she doesn't?

In many of the events listed above, two coping strategies will help. These are:

- Being prepared

- Talking through your worries with other people

The mother-to-be, for example, has nine months to prepare. Write lists of what you have to do and buy, read as much as you can in books and magazines, but most of all talk – to your partner, your doctor, your midwife, your mother, anyone you know who has ever had a baby.

Moving house is another stressful experience. Again, it is often something we very much want, have dreamed about, planned for – yet when it actually happens, we can feel ourselves getting panicky, lying awake at night, feeling as if our emotions are on a short fuse.

The advice is the same: prepare as much as you can. Write lists of everything you need to do, to remember, to organise: the solicitor, the estate agent, the removal van, the gas, the electricity, the packing, the unpacking. Write down everything as it occurs to you.

Always remember to keep to one side things you need during the move: your telephone numbers, your kettle and mugs for instant tea therapy, all the keys of everything you own, and your toothbrush, toiletries and a change of clothes. (I learned this the hard way once when I booked a removals firm to come and pack up the contents of my house. They did a brilliant job: they packed everything. I had to move house wearing high-heeled court shoes because they'd packed my trainers and it was days before I found them again!)

And talk to people. Ask advice – people usually love to give advice. You don't have to take it. But in listening to other people telling you what they think you should do, you very often work out for yourself what you don't want to do.

Stress from within

Why do some people appear to cope effortlessly with things that reduce you to a wobbling mess of emotion? (They probably don't, by the way, they just have a different way of coping).

Life, as we see from the list above, will throw plenty of stress at us. But often stress seems to come from deep within our own selves.

We all have different 'trigger points' – stressors that affect us particularly, and we all seem set with our own individual boiling points and pain thresholds.

The answer lies in the childhoods that shaped us, and the emotional baggage we carry from them. Children are like sponges: they absorb everything from the world immediately around them. They hear what their parents say, and interpret it literally. More significantly, they pick up on everything that is not said or expressed: they absorb moods, emotions, and atmospheres. They pick up on messages given to them directly ('You are a very stupid boy') and indirectly: a parent's real or imagined coldness may shape that child into his or her adult life.

The way we deal with the situations of our adult life is a direct result of the way we were dealt with when we were very small.

Psychiatrists and psychologists often come in for a lot of flak because they appear to be letting people off the hook for this reason. This is not so. If, as an adult, you behave badly in your personal or professional life it is not an excuse to blame it on your childhood.

But what unravelling the threads of your past can do is help you understand why and how you are the way you are, and in understanding there is the choice for change.

Let me give one simple example. It's often the case with adults lacking confidence that they received a message in their early childhoods that they were no good at things. 'You always make a mess of things', a parent may have said on more than one occasion. The parent may have said this because it was said to him in his own childhood - patterns like this are almost inevitably repeated again and again. That child goes to school and does not do as well as expected: this reinforces his by now internal view that he is 'no good at things'. Situations often fail because we set them up to fail and we do so because inwardly, in our deepest selves, we think that is how we are.

But who told us this? Where did it come from? The answer is that it came from a frightened, all-too-human parent who was only doing what had been done to him, reflecting the world as he saw it. Understanding the past offers the opportunity to break negative cycles and to move on in a positive way.

Stress-heightening behaviour

We also adopt behaviours or habits in life that heighten the stress we feel. These include drinking too much alcohol, drinking too much coffee, a poor diet rich in calories and sugars, and not getting enough sleep or good quality rest.

It's a point we'll come back to again but it's worth making here: any kind of stress is coped with better if you feel physically well and strong, and illness or poor health are highly stressful in themselves.

Stress is individual

Stress is personal. What stresses me may not bother you at all. For the unemployed person, stress is the daily grind of job-hunting, of living with boredom and rejection and perhaps too a sense of inferiority in a society so driven by commercialism and material values. There may also be personal feelings of failure, of having let down one's family, not to mention money worries.

Those in work are quite likely to name their job as the Number 1 cause of stress in their lives. 'If only' is a constant refrain: if only the boss wasn't such a you-know-what, if only I was paid more, if only I had more time, if only the phone didn't keep ringing, if only I could just get on with it instead of having to go to meetings all the time.

Women who work may cite sexism in the workplace as a source of stress. A woman has always had to work harder, faster and smarter than any man to get on, or even stay in the same place. Women who work and have families have an extra burden to deal with: the guilt of leaving their children while they work, the financial pressures of working to pay for the child care, exhaustion when they get home after a hard day's work and their children need their undivided attention.

Not having a family or a significant other in

your life is also stressful. The growth in dating agencies and Lonely Hearts columns (now a feature of almost every daily and evening newspaper around the country) points to a very large number of people living alone who do not want to be, and are searching for someone with whom to share their lives. We live in a world apparently designed for couples and families, when to be single can seem something of a disease to be avoided.

If only…
We may imagine it's possible to get rid of stress in our lives, but it isn't. All of us probably fantasise that our problems are nothing that can't be cured by a modest little lottery win. It's little comfort to reflect that even seriously rich people can have their problems too!

Most of us, however, do go through life playing the 'if only' game with ourselves. It goes like this: I could be happy and less stressed if only;

- I had a better job with more money
- the 8.04 train ran on time
- I could take a holiday
- I lost 20lbs
- my kids weren't so awful
- my husband understood me
- I didn't have so much to do all the time
- I didn't feel so tired all the time
- People weren't always wanting things from me

But what if nothing about your life could be changed? Let's indulge that fantasy for one moment.

Close your eyes and just think: nothing is ever going to change. You'll stay the same weight, in the same job, with the same boss, coping with daily commuter stress, never quite getting ahead of the financial demands made on you – say it loud: I am never going to win the lottery – with the same children, spouse, mother-in-law. If you're single, you are going to stay single for the rest of your life. Your cat will always be sick on that particular square of carpet. Christmas is always going to be just as dull and stressful as it is now, with members of your family being every bit as quarrelsome and cantankerous as they always have been.

Is that it, then? Does this mean you can never be happy, stress-free, contented, serene? Why not just give in and curl up your toes now?

No, no, and emphatically no.

Some years ago a BBC programme reported on a study into 'Happiness'. A group of people, who thought themselves unhappy for a variety of reasons, were followed over a six-month period during which they were taught techniques for pretending they were happy, for looking on the positive side, for trying to alter their own attitude and orient themselves towards a more contented frame of mind. At the end of six months, nothing about their personal lives had changed. The single person was still single; the person caring for an invalid relative was still 'tied' to this role. None of

them had become rich; some had become healthier,
by taking better care of their physical selves. The
only thing they had changed was their attitude. All
of them said they felt happier, and so they were.

You can't get rid of the stress in your life, but
you can get rid of the stress in you.

PERSONALITY TYPE

Why are people so different in the ways in which they cope with life? An obvious starting point is to look at the ways in which we as people are so fundamentally different from each other.

Carl Gustav Jung (1875–1961)

The most important work in this area was started by the psychoanalyst Carl Gustav Jung, a contemporary and one-time colleague of Freud, whose name will crop up many times in this book (*see* Listen to your Dreams).

Jung once wrote 'my life has been permeated by one goal...to penetrate into the secret of the personality. All my work relates to this one theme'. It was by understanding the mysteries of the human heart that Jung felt people could find fulfilment and become the fully developed people we are all born to be.

Jung's theory was that we all have a preference for a certain 'ways of being', or personality type. The key word here is 'preference' because nothing about personality is fixed or unchanging. But we do have definite tendencies and Jung defined these as:

Extrovert *or*	Introvert	How we relate to the outside world
Sensing *or*	Intuitive	How we gather and use information
Thinking *or*	Judging	How we make decisions
Feeling *or*	Perceiving	How we organise ourselves and the world

In other words, when it comes to how we relate to the world around us, people can either be extrovert (outgoing, life-and-soul-of-the-party, taking charge, perhaps bossy) or introvert (inward looking, thoughtful, focused). All the terms used above have a special meaning within Jung's theory and are not dictionary definitions, and it's important to be clear that every preference has both positive and negative aspects.

With natural extroverts, their energy flows out into the world and their environment; with introverts, their energy is contained within themselves. The world needs both types, but extroverts and introverts tend to misunderstand each other and devalue the qualities of the other. If you are a get-up-and-go type who wants to solve everything now and go out and take on the universe, you will be utterly frustrated by the thinker who wants to work everything out on paper first. Extroverts communicate with the

world; introverts communicate first with
themselves. 'Why do you never tell me anything?' is
often the cry of the exasperated extrovert to the
introvert. The introvert will communicate, but only
when he has first worked out exactly what he wants
to say, and this may take some time.

In work situations, conflict between introverts
and extroverts is almost inevitable unless they can
learn to value each other's strengths and have
patience with their very different ways of working.

In being either an extrovert or an introvert, Jung
described this as your 'attitude to the world'. The
other four types relate to functions of personality,
that is, how we operate. If in the make-up of your
personality the Thinking or the Feeling tendencies
are uppermost, then you tend to be a rational
person who evaluates things in the light of
experience: a hard facts person. If sensation or
intuition are uppermost (the so-called feminine
qualities), then you tend to trust your hunches and
your perceptions.

We've all heard conversations in which one
person yells 'but where's the evidence?' and the
other person keeps saying 'I just have this feeling
about it'. Both people in such an exchange are
being absolutely true to their personality type,
which approaches reality from the opposite

direction.

You cannot change the basic preferences of your personality, but Jung was convinced that our 'external' persona carried its 'shadow' with it. In other words, we contain our opposite qualities within ourselves – sometimes, particularly in times of stress, this shadow can become uppermost and we act 'against type'. When people who know us say things like 'I don't know what's got into you, this is not like you at all' then it's likely we are living in the shadow part of our personality.

Further reading
Maggie Hyde and Michael McGuinness, *Jung for Beginners*. Icon.
Carl Gustav Jung, Memories, *Dreams, Reflections*. Fontana.
Frieda Fordham, *An Introduction to Jung's Psychology*. Pelican.

The Myers-Briggs Type Indicator
Two admirers of Jung's work, Katharine Cook
Briggs (1875–1968) and her daughter Isabel Briggs
Myers (1897–1980) developed the Myers-Briggs
Type Indicator.

This is a written personality test in the form of a
series of questions for which you select from a
number of answers. It may be completed in about
40 minutes and, when 'marked', indicates your
personality type according to the Jungian
preferences (there are eight listed above, so 16
personality types altogether are described). More
than 3.5 million Indicators are administered
annually worldwide and used by all kinds of
institution, company and social group as tools in
understanding the people who work for them and
in helping them to understand themselves. Isabel
Myers was prompted to develop the MBTI because
of what she saw as the appalling waste of human
potential during World War II, where human
individuality was so utterly disregarded.

The MBTI is a sensitive tool, and needs to be
interpreted by a qualified professional. It is not the
kind of questionnaire you see in glossy magazines
('How ambitious are you?') and has no benefit
unless delivered by someone who can fully explain
all the various types and their implications for co-

operation or conflict. It must also be explained and emphasised that there is nothing right or wrong about any personality type; people are just different, and the MBTI seeks to celebrate that difference in unfolding it.

But once we understand that preference and personality type are an essential part of us and who we are (and that the same is true of everyone else) then it does become easier to understand why some relationships at work or in our personal lives are so stressful, why some groups of colleagues work productively together and others don't, why some situations gel and others are a disaster.

To find out more about using the MBTI in your workplace or personal life, contact Oxford Psychologists Press Limited (tel: 01865 510203). They may also be able to tell you of individual therapists in your area that administers the test.

Further reading
Isabel B. Myers with Peter Myers, *Gifts Differing: Understanding Personality Types*. Davies-Black Publishing.
Allen L. Hammer, *Introduction to Type and Careers*. Oxford Psychologists Press.

Type A and B personalities

A much cruder definition of personality was made by two American cardiologists, Friedmann and Rosenman. They noticed that many of the patients who came to them with heart attacks and other stress-related cardiovascular problems shared similar characteristics, and that these personal traits made it difficult for them to follow their doctors' advice – namely, to relax, to avoid stress, to calm down and make lifestyle changes that would hopefully avoid further cardiac emergencies.

Friedmann and Rosenman defined their 'typical' patients as Type A and reported that men (and it usually was men) with Type A characteristics were six times more likely to suffer heart attacks than Type B personalities.

You'll have noticed by now that Type A really are made to look like the bad guys, whereas all of us will rush to insist that we are Type B, who would seem to be practically saints. Basil Fawlty was clearly a Type A personality par excellence.

We need to remind ourselves again that personality is not fixed and rigid and that human beings are complex, intricate creatures capable of being many different things all at once. What is probably true is that most of us have characteristics of both Type A and Type B within us, and are capable of being either of those types at any given time.

If you do recognise parts of yourself in the Type A list, then it's almost certain that your health, your relationships and your happiness would all benefit from emphasising or trying to develop the Type B side of you.

It's evident that Type A people make their own stress: there's a voice within them saying 'Do it faster – work harder – stay later – drive yourself – go on' and that voice is something they have allowed to control their lives.

Type B's inner voice says: 'I am working to the best of my ability within the constraints of time and experience. I am a worthwhile person and I owe it to myself to look after my health and my wellbeing, to relax, to have fun and to love my life'.

Type A personalities seem to hate to play – maybe as children they were never allowed to play in that unstructured, carefree way that is important if children are to grow with a sense of the world being a good place to be, in which fun is not only possible but allowed. Type B knows that play is important because we need to rediscover our sense of fun and pleasure in the everyday.

Type A personalities	Type B personalities
Create their own stress from within themselves	Accept stress only when it comes from the world outside (see Life Events list)
Are highly competitive - winning is everything	Enjoy playing the game - winning is a bonus
Are always rushed and panic about the time available to them	Are relaxed, and thus use their time well
Are usually assertive (at best) or aggressive (at worst)	Are easy-going - not afraid to assert themselves, but never aggressive
Speak quickly and often fall over their words, explaining themselves badly	Think before they speak in clear, measured tones
Are impatient - 'why can't this be done now?'	Have a realistic attitude towards deadlines
Find relaxation impossible: a beach holiday with no mobile phone is their idea of hell	Know that relaxing well is as important as working well
Are socially inept: they hate small talk or chit-chat	Interact well with other people on several levels
Plan badly - always in a rush to do things, they don't prepare well	Are organised and make fewer mistakes
Find fault in the world around them and are often eager to apportion blame	Accept the world as it is, and know that blame is a useless indulgence
Feel they are what they do and they can only earn respect by doing it better than anyone else	Don't feel they have to prove anything - they are secure in their own sense of self-worth
Are easily bored and have short attention spans	Take pleasure in the here and now, and the small things of life - good food, good company, walks in the country
Believe the more they acquire the happier they will be	Want to 'live' not 'have'

Whenever you feel that your Type A has the upper hand, tell that inner voice to be quiet for a moment and let the good common sense of Type B take over. There is no evidence that Type B does not get the job done just as well or as fast or as effectively as Type A: there is only evidence that Type A is dreaded by his colleagues and has the heart attack, while Type B is having a good time somewhere else.

Further reading
Patricia Hodges, *Understanding your Personality.* Sheldon Press.
Paul Hauck, *Calm Down.* Sheldon Press.

Are men and women different in response to stress?
Probably. A typical effect of stress is to make us
feel that we are being drowned or suffocated by the
number of demands made on us. Typically, women
are more used to multiple and conflicting demands
than men, and better at coping with them.

When women's sole occupation was running the
home, they were used to a variety of tasks that had
to be done at different times: cooking, cleaning,
shopping, gardening, running a chauffeur service
for the children. They adjusted to the fact that one
job can seldom be finished properly because
another one, more urgent, is screaming for
attention. Motherhood by its very nature
encourages women to be flexible, responsive to the
moment, and adaptable – all qualities that help in
the management of stress.

It's also a sad fact that women have often been
brought up not to have their needs met. In her
excellent book *What do Women Want?* Susie
Orbach theorises that women bring up their
daughters to nurture and nourish others (quite
literally, as they are traditionally in charge of the
food) while the sons are brought up to be looked
after. First of all boys are cared for by their
mothers, then sisters, then girlfriends, wives and
perhaps eventually daughters. Girls are brought up

to do the caring: they cope, because that's what women do.

It follows then have men have high expectations of life in terms of what it will give them; women don't, because it is generally their role to make sure other people are looked after first. It is no accident that the so-called caring professions – nursing, teaching, social work – are dominated by women, though when it comes to being managers or making the decisions in those professions, a small group of men-at-the-top suddenly emerge to take charge.

This pattern is society is changing, but it does explain why women cope with stress better than men. There are other reasons, too.

One is that women talk to each other more. They maintain family ties and they build up networks of friendship and when women talk, they talk. Sure, they'll talk about supposedly trivial things like clothes and hair and diets, but women typically have few inhibitions about talking about how they rally feel, what their relationships are like, the state of their emotions. They freely acknowledge that they have an inner emotional life and that this life must be paid attention to.

Men, brought up (again typically, and again this is changing) to be tough and strong and 'real boys', do not open themselves to each other or to anyone else emotionally. They can often pretend emotions don't exist. The chat can be football or money or cars or antique furniture but it will seldom be 'how I really feel when the boss hauls me over the coals' or 'how I really feel about being a husband and father'.

Starting with Freud, the founding father of psychoanalysis, therapists have known that emotions that don't get acknowledged do not go away. Just because you never ever talk about your inner life does not mean you don't have one, or that it will eventually just give up and perish for lack of attention. The opposite tends to happen, in fact. The suppressed inner self breaks out of its prison in all sorts of ways we find inconvenient or unhelpful – psychosomatic illnesses, for example, are just one way in which our real self can call out for attention.

In our culture, many if not most men are deeply uncomfortable talking about their emotions or their inner world. They feel utterly embarrassed and inadequate when they hear phrases like 'emotional literacy' or 'emotional intelligence'.

Yet these very men may be the ones to suffer most from stress-related illnesses or conditions such as psoriasis, eczema or asthma, these men may be the ones most at risk of hypertension or heart attacks, they may be the ones who suffer most from the ageing effects of stress at work and poor relationships in their personal lives – the typical Type A personality.

Whatever small steps men (and women) can take to acknowledge the reality of their emotional lives is a bonus for them.

The second reason why women tend to respond better to stress is their willingness to seek relaxation in beneficial therapies. The huge rise of complementary therapies such as acupuncture and aromatherapy in recent years has been overwhelmingly driven by women. Utterly disenchanted with the male-dominated, mechanical and often anti-women attitude of the medical profession, women have found that complementary therapies do just as their name implies and complement their lives, that is, enhance them, make them richer.

The stereotypical stressed male heads to the pub and seeks stress relief in alcohol. Now that there are more women in competitive jobs they, too, often adopt male patterns of stress relief.

It would be good if men could follow the lead given by women and open their minds (if not their wallets) and explore a few complementary therapies. Not because they are necessarily the answer, but because many of them do offer genuine relaxation and release in a stressful world.

Further reading
Luise Eichenbaum and Susie Orbach, *What do Women Want?* HarperCollins.

Control, control, control

'Control freak' is a commonly used expression these days. When we describe others as control freaks, they tend to be people whom we don't like very much. It is very often used about people in authority over us such as managers. When we describe ourselves as control freaks, however, it tends to be with a rueful laugh; we think if we get in there first and admit it, we'll spare other people having to do it behind our backs.

The control freak manager is the manager who would actually like to do your job as well as his or her own, just to make sure it is done properly (that is, as he or she thinks it should be done). The CFM is first in the building in the morning, leaves last thing at night, is perpetually anxious about things other people can shrug off, and will go through your in-tray when you're on holiday or ill, just to check there is nothing happening he or she does not know about.

The CFM is a very bad manager because what he likes to manage is things not people. You don't have to relate to a set of figures, there's no need to make eye contact or small talk with a sales chart. Things can be controlled, of course (or so we like to think) but people can't.

Control freaks do not just like their homes to be

perfectly organised and efficiently run – they need them to be that way. They are deeply and genuinely upset by untidiness or chaos, even when that apparent chaos is creative – for example, a kitchen while a meal is being cooked. The control freak wipes and washes as she goes, and a home with small children in it – who typically like to play and leave their toys scattered everywhere in no particular order – can be very stressful for the CF. Control freaks designate days of the week for particular tasks and hate disruption to routine. The unexpected guest who just drops by, the impromptu party organised by neighbours ('Fancy only deciding to do it now! Why can't they have done all this weeks ago!'), the spur-of-the-moment holiday are all things that never happen in the life of the CF.

The control freak may be convinced there is a worldwide conspiracy against them, and that there is a party happening this weekend to which everyone has been invited except for them. The first is paranoia, of course, but the second may well, in extreme cases, be true.

Pity this poor person, because all of us have the tendency to a greater or lesser degree. If we step back from the stereotype for a moment and examine the reality, we can see that all the qualities

UNDERSTANDING STRESS

Where the control freak focuses	An alternative (less stressful) focus
Food: the CF usually has an uneasy relationship with food, trying to control intake and weight in ways which may ultimately lead to illness	Focus on achieving optimum health and wellbeing, not weight and calories
Fitness: 'I must do a 40-minute run every day, no matter how tired I am'	As above: What's important is that I'm healthy and well - other goals take second place to that
Work: 'if only people would do what I tell them!'	I manage my staff as well as I can, and I try to choose the best people for the job, but it's their job - not mine. I explain, I delegate, and I leave them alone to do it. My door is always open to them
I never know where my teenage daughter is, she just ignores me	She knows I am always there to love and support her, but she needs to find her own life, and I need to develop a life of my own post-children
The kids leave their toys all over the place, I can't stand it	Children need their own space to play creatively and, yes, messily. I'm going to give them their space to do this, and not attempt to control it, but insist that they respect other areas of the house where my standards of tidiness apply
I need to keep everything under control so that other people will like me	I like myself, so it doesn't matter so much what other people think of me. I please myself first
I work as hard as I can so the boss will approve of me	I take pleasure in my job for its own sake and want to fulfil my own potential
I have to earn as much money as possible to stave off my inner feelings of inadequacy	I know that material things won't necessarily make me happy and that quality of life is more important

negatively associated with the control freak are a way of coping with stress.

At the risk of stating the obvious, the world is generally beyond our control. It has always been a place where random and often dreadful things happen – wars, accidents, natural disasters such as earthquakes – but because of television and newspapers and the Internet we have never been so powerfully aware of what is out there and how frightening it can be.

Even those who think they are in charge, such as political leaders, and who generally exhibit the very worst tendencies of control freakery, really aren't. The world is much too complex for anyone, even the President of the United States, to actually control very much of it at all.

Recent decades have brought their own particular terrors to keep us awake, from the threat of global warming and environmental destruction to nuclear warfare and, more locally, massive unemployment and financial insecurity. Yet we are, most of us, very much better off financially and in terms of material goods than our parents dreamed of being and our children in turn have grown up expecting as their right things we had never seen, like computers.

A headline in *The Independent* on 15 September

1999 read 'Britain in 2010: rich but far too stressed to enjoy it'. A report commissioned by the Salvation Army found that increased material prosperity has not brought happiness. On the contrary, many of those interviewed for the study felt that work and career demands had dominated their lives to such an extent that they had significantly lost out in other areas – most notably, seeing their children grow up, or in developing and maintaining satisfying relationships.

'All sectors of society', the article said, 'are suffering from the modern social condition – loneliness, stress and a deteriorating quality of life'.

We have so much that we're afraid of losing, and it is perhaps that fear and insecurity that makes us cling even harder to the idea that we are – or can be – in control.

The tragic rise in incidence of eating disorders such as anorexia nervosa and bulimia has been seen as attempts to control the uncontrollable. When women feel they are not in charge of their own lives, what can they control? In many cases exerting an inflexible control over what they eat (or don't) gives an illusion of being powerful rather than powerless.

Yet we are not helpless. The truth is that in our own part of the world we are, still, in charge of our

daily lives and we can all make choices about the
way we live and behave. The secret is to know what
you can take charge of, and what you can't. In the
words of the 'Serenity prayer', we need to change
those things we can, and accept those things we
can't – and have the wisdom to know the
difference.

What's the difference between an organised, tidy
person (*see* Organisation) and a control freak?
Typically, control freaks choose all the wrong
things to try and control: other people, their
children, the world at large. They fail, or at least
perceive that these things are slipping from their
grasp, and become increasingly frustrated and thus
more determined to try and control their
environment. This is when the shoes get re-
ordered in the wardrobe in colour order and the
sweaters re-folded in tissue paper. (Please don't
think I'm mocking control freaks: we all have these
tendencies within us).

The only way out of this vicious cycle is to re-
focus on things that can be changed and in 99% of
cases the answer will be: only myself.

Here are some examples of ways in which we
can learn to adjust our focus to what can be done,
rather than what can't.

Change your mind, and your life will change itself
Remember that list you made earlier, of the five things that caused you stress in your life?

Look at it again, remembering the words from the Serenity Prayer: God grant me the courage to change those things I can, the serenity to accept those things I can't, and the wisdom to know the difference.

What category do the things you've written on your list fall into? Things you can change could be any or all of the following:

- Your job
- Your lifestyle
- Your relationship (that is, the quality of it, if not the relationship itself!)

Things you probably can't change include:

- Other people in your life
- Your health
- Your age

It's sometimes difficult to categorise things that neatly. You can't change your health if you are suffering from a chronic or long-term medical condition, but there may be things you can do to improve it, and to increase your sense of wellbeing. You can't change the age you are, but by improving your health and stimulating your mind you may well start to feel younger.

You can't change other people in your life in the sense of altering their personalities to suit you, but if, for example, you feel that you spend too much time with a group of people whose influence on your life you feel to be negative, then you can do something about that. It tends to be the case that we subconsciously seek out companions who reinforce our own attitude to life, whether that is negative or positive. Ask yourself whether the people with whom you choose to pass your leisure time have a 'yes' or a 'no' attitude. Do you sit around complaining about everything that is bad, and wrong, or looking for things to laugh about that are good, and pleasurable? If you want to be the kind of person who loves life, you don't need to carry a bunch of doom merchants around in your address book.

Family relationships come into the category of things we can't change. Yet very often a change in our own attitude can appear to alter everything. A friend of mine, for instance, has a sister-in-law who induced feelings of inferiority in my friend – let's call her Maggie. It occurred to Maggie to wonder why this was so, and she realised that she (Maggie) probably had exactly the same effect on the sister-in-law. Each woman, trying to cope with her own feelings of inadequacy when faced with a totally different personality type, withdrew into 'protective hostility'. Difficult relationships with other people often stem from the fact that we look at the surface behaviour (often a mass of protective emotional barbed wire) and don't see the real person. This insight helped Maggie to feel more confident and herself in her sister-in-law's company, and to relax instead of feeling 'got at'.

Carl Gustav Jung wrote a lot about 'projection'. When another person arouses strong feelings of hostility or anxiety in you, look at that person closely. When you find yourself lashing out at the 'thoughtless, selfish' behaviour of someone else, take note of what that behaviour is. Jung's theory is that our strong reactions are because we recognise an aspect of ourselves and our behaviour in other people.

If you think your job is the main source of stress in your life, the obvious answer is to change it. And, if you can, why not? Americans – who have enshrined the inalienable right to the pursuit of happiness in their Constitution – would have no such qualms. You don't like a situation, you just pack up and move on. There's a healthy spark in that that we should all admire and applaud.

But before you do, just pause a moment to reflect whether the stress you feel in your job comes from the job itself – or from within you. Does the stress descend the minute you enter your office, and lift the minute you leave? Is it to do with the job itself and the nature of the work, or is it perhaps because you have a difficult relationship with colleagues or your boss?

If you can definitely say that your stress is wholly because of the job then have no hesitation in making every effort to move on.

If you think some at least of the stress comes from you then remember that 'a different address may only land you in a different kind of mess'. Your problems with the boss, for instance – perhaps you have a general difficulty with authority? Perhaps you find it difficult to take orders, or respect the judgement of others? Try to solve your problems with stress first, and then move on.

Catastrophising

Do you know the advertising slogan that says 'we don't make a drama out of a crisis'? Many of us do that all the time, creating our own high stress levels. It's called catastrophising.

Catastrophising is when we take 'ordinary' everyday events that go wrong (or even slightly askew) and blow them up out of all proportion. A missed appointment sends your heart-rate pounding. A red traffic light sends you into a rage.

Look again at that list of 'life events' said to be stressful. If we're honest, only a handful – bereavement, for example, or the break-up of a personal relationship – may be said to be always stressful. Some of the others are stressful simply because we allow them to be: in stress as in everything else in life, there is an element of choice. We can choose not to be stressed.

Why would people catastrophise? The generation that lived through World War II, for example, would say 'they don't know what stress is'. Even today, all over the world, people are living through genuinely horrific times – yet we get stressed because of rush-hour traffic.

One possible answer is that the focus of our lives is too narrow. We forget that we are part of a wider society and beyond that, the brotherhood of mankind. It's as if there is a spotlight on us and our lives and the wider world beyond is in darkness.

Another possible answer (which may appear contradictory but isn't) is that we don't focus enough on the present moment. Our brains race like over-heated engines, living in the future (*see* Mindfulness).

It's important that we see the events of our lives in proportion, and don't waste energy in needless anxieties over small things – and as Richard Carlson says in his eloquent book title (see below), it's almost all small stuff.

Further reading
Richard Carlson, *Don't sweat the small stuff - and it's all small stuff.* Hodder and Stoughton.

About this book

This book will not remove stress from your life. Stress is a necessary, integral and healthy part of the way we are. But unnecessary stress, or the inability to cope effectively with long periods of stress, is a killer. Literally. People die of heart attacks and they die, sadly, of other illnesses caused or heightened by stress. Equally tragically, many people take their own lives each year as a way of ending stress.

What I hope this book will do, as the title implies, is help you to understand stress – and the key to doing that is always a better understanding of ourselves. When we know ourselves a little better, we can begin to feel empowered to take charge of our own lives and feelings.

Part 2 of this book looks at psychotherapy and counselling as ways of dealing with stress. Not everyone will want to go off and book a session with a therapist, and that's fine. Therapy is not necessarily the answer, but good therapy can offer us a way of seeing ourselves in a different light, of understanding some of the reasons why we are as we are, why we behave as we do.

To give one example: someone who has immense problems at work with authority, with the boss, with those who appear to have power in such situations, may find in therapy that this relates to difficulties with figures who were in authority in his or her childhood. We don't leave our childhoods behind: they still live inside us, powerful inhibitors or motivators. The child who was repeatedly told 'Don't touch that, you always break things' is probably now the frightened adult scared of seeking fulfilment because he will 'break things'.

Formal counselling is not the only way of looking inside ourselves. There have never been more self-help books on the market purporting to offer insights into human behaviour, and at least some of these can really help.

Stress may not always be cured, but it can be coped with. There are a whole host of relaxation techniques that can help us to calm down, to focus, to breathe more deeply, to feel better, to live in the here and now. In the final section of the book we look at some of these, including yoga, aromatherapy, reflexology and the Alexander Technique.

If you're reading this book, it's probably because you feel under stress yourself, and feel that your life is not as good as it could be as a result. Stress can be very isolating – it's important to know that you are not alone.

A word about practitioners
As a result of reading this book, or perhaps because you already wanted to, you may want to go out and contact a therapist or a reflexologist or a teacher of Alexander Technique.

There are national bodies in the UK for most complementary therapies and a list of addresses is given at the end. As a first port of call, you may want to contact them and ask for a list of practitioners in your area and for their recommendations on price per session (which can vary widely). Your local health food store is also usually a good place to spot advertisements, or try the library.

And, as with anything in life from finding a hairdresser to a plumber or a neurosurgeon, personal recommendation from someone whose judgement you trust is invaluable.

But remember that complementary therapies are not yet bound by statutory regulations concerning quality and competence. The national bodies themselves all want this, as they want to protect the reputations of the genuine therapist from the damage done by the bogus. But at the moment the fact is that anyone can put a plaque on their door and call themselves almost any kind of therapist or practitioner.

A genuine practitioner will have trained with some recognised national body and will be proud to display their certificates. They will be upfront about fees, terms and conditions. The best therapists will not take on a client without a frank discussion about what the client wants and expects, and what the therapist is offering. The best therapists will make eye contact, treat you with respect, and honour their commitments to you.

Trust your instinct and walk out of any situation in which you do not feel comfortable. Any psychotherapist or counsellor who tries to give advice, or tell you what to do, or who starts a sentence with 'Your problem is...' should be given a wide berth. They are not there to give you an agenda for changing your life, they are there to listen constructively and empathically and to support you as you sort through your own issues.

Let's go on now and look at ways of starting to explore our inner selves, where stress can begin to accumulate.

PART 2
HEALING FROM WITHIN

We've agreed that there is not much you can do to stop life throwing stressful events at you. What you can do, however, is choose how to deal with those stresses. There are things you can do for yourself, and things where you need the help of a third party - 'an empathic listener' such as a counsellor or therapist.

THINGS YOU CAN DO FOR YOURSELF

Goal setting

Happy people have been defined as people with goals in life. It follows, obviously, that not having goals of any kind make you unhappy – and they certainly make you stressed. Without organisation in your life there is muddle, and muddle has a way of spreading until it seems like a layer of dust covering everything around you.

Give yourself time to sit down, alone and quiet, and doodle on a piece of paper. Just what are your goals? Many people under acute stress find it hard enough to get through the next hour, let alone the next month, so break your goals down into manageable chunks. Have goals for:

- Today
- This week
- This month

Don't think beyond that if you can't. When people are suffering a bereavement, for example, or the distress of a marital breakup, it is best not to think too far ahead. Friends may rally round and say 'One day, this will all just be a memory' but that is not actually comforting or useful in the here and now. What matters to the distressed person is now, today.

Don't set unrealistic goals. Set goals that are within your financial and physical means of achieving. Learning French, for instance – something you've always wanted to do – is not realistic if you have neither the time nor the motivation, and the only really good motivation might be the fact that you're going to live there next month. Examples of short-term goals that will nevertheless give you a sense of achievement once they're accomplished can include very simple things:

● Phone a friend or relative you've been meaning to chat to for ages

● Have a hair cut or a beauty treatment

● Go and see a film or a play or read a book that people have been talking about

● Do some niggling task you've been putting off –letters to your bank, insurance renewals, checking your pension statements, and so on

● Book a holiday for six weeks' time – it doesn't need to be a week abroad; a weekend in a luxury hotel or a good bed and breakfast in Britain will do; the point is it has to be a treat for you

A clear set of goals you feel comfortable with should also be sub-divided into goals connected with your personal life and your working life.

At work, most of us have our goals set for us by other people, by our managers. We have targets and performance indicators and assessment reviews – but these are all imposed on you and consist largely of what others think of you. Do you have your own goals in your working life? These might include:

● Skills I want to acquire, such as new computer skills

● Other parts of the company for which I would like to work – can you talk to your Human Resources manager about this?

● The type of job I would like to be doing in five years' time

● If you don't want to change your present job, can you think of ways in which you could work better, more effectively?

But don't think of goal setting only in terms of your career, and the plans that you have for your working life. Your personal life needs just as much attention, if not more. If your personal life is in good shape you will have more energy and drive and that will spill over into your working environment. Sadly, the reverse is almost never true: people who work hard to be successful from nine to five seldom bring the good parts of that home with them. I've known people who are excellent managers in their day jobs but fail to see that those same qualities (courtesy, being a good listener, getting back to people on action points you have promised to deal with) would benefit them when they interact with the supermarket checkout person or even with their own family.

Look at your personal life as if it's made up of three components:

● Where you live: that is, your flat or house, as well as the area

● Your finances

● Your social life (which includes, of course, your Relationship with a capital R or lack of it)

If two out of those three are OK, you're a lucky person. But if you look at each of those individual areas and feel things are not so good, then it's time to sit down and set some goals for improving them.

If you feel stressed because your personal life seems to be a muddle, it's important to realise that you can't tackle everything at once. If you're feeling lonely living in a grim flat with an overdraft at the bank, don't feel that all of these problems can be solved at once – though I hope they can. Tackle one thing at a time, and start with the easiest, whichever one that is.

Free financial advice can be found from many sources, for instance, starting with the local Citizens' Advice Bureau, or even your own bank. Many CABs now employ specialist debt counsellors. You're not alone in getting into financial difficulties and it is certainly not a crime. But neither is it a hopeless situation. You do need to sit down with a pencil and paper and work out what you earn – and can you improve on that? Get an evening job in a pub or restaurant, for instance? – and what you spend, and what you can sensibly cut down on. Don't panic and say 'I will give up drink and cigarettes and stay in every night' because that's not realistic. If cigarettes and going out with your friends are the mainstays of your life at the moment, you are unlikely to stick to any plan of action that involves cutting them out all at once.

Once you have a plan of action for getting your

finances into better shape, tackle the next item on your list, and so on.

Once you've ticked some of the short-term goals off your list, plan for the medium term – say six months' time – and then eventually for the long term, five or ten years. Don't try to do this too soon when you're not feeling ready for it, but it has been said that the happiest people have a ready supply of goals in all three categories.

For example:

● Short term goals – getting the grass cut, inviting Sid and Sam to supper, tidying out the hall cupboard

● Medium term goals – saving for a holiday, decorating the spare bedroom, stencilling a chest of drawers, getting fit, taking up a new interest, going to the movies more often

● Long term goals – moving house, retiring early, changing career in mid-life, writing a novel

A philosopher once wrote 'The only joy in life is to begin'. There's no greater misery than feeling helpless and overwhelmed by circumstances that appear to be out of control. There is a great pleasure to be had, by contrast, with making plans for yourself to improve the quality of your own life.

Organisation

I'm not a naturally tidy person and my working desk always looks as if a wind-machine has been turned on nearby. I'm also one of those cooks who is most comfortable when the kitchen resembles the scene of a Mafia assassination.

But I write from the heart when I say that one instant and immediate stress-buster is to get yourself organised. Someone once described a house as a machine for living in, and machines work best when things are in the right place, functioning properly. Every so often I have to take a day to work from top to bottom and put everything back in its right place, tidying as I go, and I have to say it gives me a tremendous feel of achievement. The stress lifts with every piece of junk mail I tear up and throw out, with every six-month-old magazine I consign to the bucket.

Sorting out the junk mail can become a metaphor for sorting out the junk in your mind. For instance, as you throw away things you no longer need or want, think of attitudes in your mind that slow you down and that you no longer need or want. Do you still harbour resentment because of a past wrong that you feel was done to you? Are you still jealous of someone in your partner's past? Do you still fret for a romance that went wrong but, you feel, could have been The One? Do you still agonise over a job you didn't get, an opportunity that came to nothing? You can do nothing productive about such thoughts, because their time is past. Your time is now. Tear up these going-nowhere thoughts, and throw them out with the junk mail.

We all lead such busy lives that it's hard enough getting from day to day while the mail piles up and the list of Things to Do gets longer. But if we leave things long enough then chaos becomes its own stress.

And when I say get organised I mean really organised. Don't just buy a diary, use it. Don't straighten the magazines on the coffee table, go through the pile and throw out what you don't want. Don't re-order the shoes in your wardrobe in colour order, ask yourself which ones you never ever wear and take them to the charity shop. The American philosopher Thoreau wrote: 'Our life is frittered away by detail – simplify, simplify'. The fashion for feng shui seems to be based on nothing more complicated that a good old-fashioned clear out, and making the best use of uncluttered space.

But it's not just your house and your desk and your kitchen cupboards, it's your life too. A management consultant once gave a good piece of advice for the workplace: always leave your desk at night as if you're just off on a three-week holiday. In other words, if you got run over by a bus on the way home, would it be absolutely clear to other people what was going on?

Morbid as this may sound; it's not a bad idea in your personal life to think occasionally that you could get run over by a bus tomorrow. First, you will really appreciate today a whole lot more, and value what the present moment gives you. Secondly, it will make you focus on the order in which your personal life is. Are all your bills paid? Have you made a will? Is your insurance adequate and up to date? Are all your important documents such as insurance certificates and pension records in one place, labelled and in order, so that if need be someone else could find their way through them?

It's to be hoped that the day on which your loved ones have to tidy up the business of your life is a very long way away, but it's good for us all to focus here and now on the kind of order in which we keep our lives.

Listen to your dreams

As the section on sleep says later on in this book, many of the stressful events in life can seem a whole lot less desperate if you have had a restful night's sleep; many quite trivial incidents can blow up out of all proportion if you are jagged after a restless night.

But quality sleep is important for one other reason, and that is your dreams. We need to dream: the act of dreaming is a kind of mental thermostat acting on the issues of the day and our lives, and if sleep is troubled or disturbed then dreams can't do their work.

Ancient cultures valued and feared dreams, knowing they were significant and believing they had the power to foretell the future – as in the story of Joseph from the Bible. Priests or shamans who could interpret dreams were powerful figures. In our more sceptical age, the tendency is to regard dreams as weird, sometimes entertaining but fundamentally meaningless pictures we see in our heads at night: cheese and heavy meals eaten late at night are thought to be a cause of dreams, as if somehow they were a function of the digestive system. One of the more damaging side-effects of sleeping pills over a long period of time is that they inhibit dreaming, thus robbing the sleepless person of a link with their subconscious.

Whatever may or may not affect dreaming, their importance in our psychological health is becoming better understood. The psychoanalyst Carl Gustav Jung made a lifelong study of dreams and their meaning; he worked with his patients through their dreams, believing that the dreams revealed things the patients themselves could not, because dreams are our subconscious mind communicating directly with us.

When the body goes to sleep, the mind does not. In dreams, the mind continues to work: on the issues of the day, on issues connected with the dreamer's life, on problems and challenges. If you cannot remember your dreams, the theory is that this is because they have done their work. In the dream state, issues are resolved and dealt by with the subconscious; they can then be safely stored away.

We remember dreams when they have not done their work, when the issue remains unresolved, when the difficulty or problem remains.

It is very helpful, if you want to work with your dreams, to keep a diary of them. Because dreams are so easily forgotten, it's as well to keep this in two ways: always have a pen and jotter by your bed, so that you can scrawl down what you remember as you wake in note form, for instance 'Dark – candle – Jack in top hat – raining outside' and so on. Then when you are fully awake in the morning, write up these notes in a notebook, trying to remember as much as you can of the dream. It's important that you write down every detail that you remember, even if it seems absurd; it's also very important that you don't try and manipulate the dream so that it makes sense, or makes a logical 'story'. If it seems disjointed and fragmentary, then that may be a part of what it is trying to say.

The 'problem' with dreams is, of course, that they so often seem bizarre, meaningless and confused. But if you maintain a faithful record of them, not skewing your memory in any way, and can look back over months and years of remembered dreams, a pattern will emerge and become clear to you.

Dreams have a language of their own, which is why they can seem so obscure to us. They are not logical or rational – why does Auntie Mildred keep an elephant in a glass case? Why is my son riding a penny farthing? But dreams don't have to obey the rules of 'normal' life: they come from our subconscious, that intuitive, unfettered labyrinth that is not ordered and rational as we believe everyday life (and our conscious mind) to be. To expect dreams to make obvious sense is like expecting a *Marx Brothers* film to be serious.

When it comes to interpreting your dreams, patience is required. The language of our dreams is as individual and personal as we are, and often it's only in understanding ourselves more, and gaining a more distant perspective on these dreams, that we can find an answer to their meaning. I have myself kept a dream diary going back some ten years or more. I can look back to a period when I was in a very bad relationship, which was coming unglued (though in my conscious mind I refused to see this). At the time, I had two or three vivid, powerful and distressing dreams from which I awoke in a very emotional state. At the time, I could make no sense of them. My conscious mind was so 'blocked' to what was happening that I could not (would not) see what the dreams were trying to say. Re-reading those dreams years later, their meaning seems to be crystal clear.

There are books on the market which claim to be dictionaries of dreams. Most of these contain a grain of sense, some are patently ludicrous. I opened one at random and read that if you dream of a cupboard it means you will marry a joiner who will keep you poor but happy!

That said, most therapists who work with

dreams see patterns re-occurring and can pinpoint certain symbols that are seen again and again. For instance, to dream of a house is usually to dream of your own psyche or personality, with the cellar or basement being your subconscious and the public rooms of the house representing your conscious self. Water is also said to represent sexuality.

The more stress we are under, the more our dreams will work for us. (It's important, as I said above, to avoid sleeping pills if you can, as these will prevent you dreaming; alcohol can have the same effect). If you want to try and interpret what they are saying, approach them in the same way as you would a cryptic crossword puzzle. The clue should not be taken at face value; the clue aims to deceive, so that you miss the real meaning of the question. Lateral thinking is called for. Exactly the same 'free thought' is called for when you look at your dreams.

Sit with the dream written in front of you, and a blank sheet of paper. Use the paper for a brainstorming session in which you write down, randomly, any associations you can think of with the colours, sounds and images of the dream. Forget the 'story line' but look at the images. Do these images have any special significance for you? Can you remember other instances in your waking or dreaming life when you saw these images? What did people in your dream say – the exact words are significant? One therapist was able to help a patient with a dream when she remembered that a character had actually said 'It's the time which counts' and not 'It's time that matters'. The 'which counts' was highly significant in the context of the dream.

Remember also that, as in crossword puzzles, you can be deceived by the sound of words. If you wake up hearing the words 'Which tyres?' over and over again in your mind (and you may actually have seen car tyres), remember it could also mean 'Witch tires'.

This is not quick work, though you will become fluent in the language of your dreams just as you can become fluent in any other language – with practice.

Many psychotherapists are interested in dream interpretation and happy to work with clients on their dream diaries, particularly if those therapists have trained in Jungian analysis. Even if you don't want to enter into a formal therapy relationship, you may still find therapists to work on your dreams alone.

Writing your way clear

If you have made a habit of writing a diary or keeping a personal notebook, you already have a source of instant stress relief to hand – literally.

Writing it all down, just how you feel, your thoughts, your true feelings, your emotions – all of this can be an immense release. In many ways writing is better than talking to someone else: no friend could be expected to deal with the levels of emotion you truly feel and need to express. When we talk to others, whether they are friends or therapists, we all tend to step into a role. Most of us mask our feelings to a greater or lesser extent and indeed in society it is probably necessary for us to do this at times.

But there's nothing between you and a sheet of paper and a notebook. It is utterly private and utterly confidential and safe. You can tear it up the minute you've written it.

Once, when I was at a very low point in my life, a counsellor suggested I write a letter to myself of exactly how I felt at that moment. Then, she said, seal the envelope and put it away for six months. Of course I forgot all about it, so it was about a year before I came across the envelope and read the letter I had written to myself. I was amazed at the grief and anger this person felt: emotions I could by then but dimly remember.

But the point about times of great stress or distress is that we feel trapped in the present, and in the misery of this particular moment. Write exactly how you feel, and promise yourself to look at this again in a few hours, or days, or weeks, or months. There will be a change, a shift, as the days and the weeks pass.

If writing for yourself seems to miss the point, then write letters to other people in your life – but don't post them. A woman I know, who was going through a very painful divorce, felt a great deal of bottled-up anger towards her estranged husband. She found it helpful to express her feelings in the form of a series of letters to him, which she then put in a shoebox at the back of a cupboard. There was nothing to be gained by sending them – he wasn't about to change his attitudes or behaviour – but she needed to express how she really felt. Three years later, and happy in a new relationship, she was amazed at what she'd written, and happy enough to donate the letters to the bonfire. They had served their purpose.

A study in the *Journal of the American Medical Association* found that sufferers, whether they were suffering mentally or physically, who wrote about their problems improved twice as quickly as other patients. The report concluded that 'it is possible that the writing task changed the way people thought and remembered previous stressful events in their lives and helped them cope with new events'.

Writing is a therapeutic activity for body as well as mind. Research has shown that in the act of writing the body calms, the pulse slows and breathing becomes more regular.

Louise DeSalvo, author of *Writing as a Way of Healing*, says it's important not to censor what you write (so make sure you keep your notebook in a very safe place if you don't want others to see it) and not to make your writing an essay in self-pity. 'What you record shouldn't be a litany of moans about a dreadful day. You describe what you feel and take a step back: you try to achieve some wisdom about it'. In other words, writing gives some immediate perspective on your experiences.

Be aware, too, that what comes out may even startle or alarm you: you may have a need to express deep emotions you did not know were there. But this is the story of your life, your heritage, and you can feel proud that you are starting to tell it.

Further reading
Louise De Salvo, *Writing as a Way of Healing.* The
Women's Press.

Breathing

One sure way of telling how stressed someone is, is by their breathing. When stressed our breath becomes shallower and more rapid, a quick intake of breath that comes from the upper body.

The old custom of saying 'Take a deep breath and count to ten' to someone who appears about to explode with pent-up feelings is actually helpful advice. In moments of immediate stress, concentrate on your breathing, as this can rapidly calm tense muscles and nerves.

Real breathing is through the nostrils, not the mouth. Often when people make a conscious effort to breathe deeply they puff their chests up and breathe from the chest, but for maximum benefit we should breathe from our diaphragms. Really deep breathing (such as we do when exerting ourselves in exercise) assists in the process of releasing endorphins, the body's natural stress-relievers.

To check that you are breathing from your diaphragm, do this: place your hands on your hips, with your thumb resting in the little hollow just above the hip bone and your fingers spread across your tummy. Take a deep breath – but don't force it - and keep your shoulders and your chest as still as possible. Your shoulders should not move when you breathe. Now as you slowly breathe in and out feel your tummy fill and move out and in with your breathing.

The study of yoga places great emphasis on correct breathing, so if stress affects you by making your breathing effortful and shallow, some yoga classes could help.

Alternate nostril breathing.
One yoga technique recommended for stress is alternate nostril breathing.

1. Place the index and middle fingers of your right hand in the middle of your forehead, between your eyebrows.

2. Your thumb should be on your right nostril, and your ring and little fingers on the left one. (Don't worry if you can't move both these fingers together, you will with practice).

3. Press your thumb against your right nostril, and slowly breathe in and out only through the left.

4. Then close your left nostril with your little finger, and do the same.

5. Repeat this several times in an unhurried manner, concentrating on your breathing.

Being assertive

People who find it difficult to be assertive often find themselves under a great deal of stress. Assertion means having the ability to express your wishes and your needs clearly to other people, and to stand your ground calmly and without anger in situations of conflict. If you find it hard to do this, you may find yourself swept along by other people's wishes and by events you want no part of.

Lack of assertiveness can come from low self-esteem or a lack of self-confidence, and even relatively trivial situations can become major crises if you cannot deal with them assertively. For instance, if an acquaintance asks you for a favour which you really don't want to do, but you cannot just say 'no', then the stress of having been inveigled into a situation where you have an unwanted obligation is immensely stressful.

It's important to be clear from the outset that assertiveness is not the same as aggression, and aggressive people are not assertive – they're just bullies. Assertiveness is not about anger or expressing anger, though un-assertive people themselves often feel a great deal of unexpressed anger. Superficially, they probably feel angry with others for 'making me do things'; subconsciously, they are frustrated and angry with themselves for not feeling able to say what they want.

The first step on the road to assertiveness is an expression of your personal rights. You need to accept that you have as much right as everyone else to certain things. These are:

1. I have the right to ask for what I want in life (and other people also have the right to say 'no').

2. I am a person with opinions, feelings and emotions and I have the right to express these when I see fit.

3. I have the right to say 'yes' or 'no' for myself alone – I don't speak for other people and I don't expect them to speak for me.

4. I have the right to say 'I don't understand' and ask for clarification.

5. I have the right to change my mind at any time.

6. I am not responsible for other people's happiness or unhappiness.

7. I have the right to my own privacy, and to choose with whom to share my private moments.

8. I have the right not to explain myself when I have expressed a personal view about something.

9. I have the right to make mistakes, and to learn from them.

10. Just as I feel it is my right to be respected as an autonomous individual, so I will respect all others with whom I come into contact.

Learning to be assertive can be a slow and painful business. Many of us grew up fearing anger and disapproval, and wanting to please, and this can lie at the heart of our problems with assertiveness. If you grew up in a household where phrases similar to these could be heard;

● Just wait until Daddy gets home and I tell him what you've done

● Be a good girl/boy and Daddy/Mummy will be pleased

● What a good boy! You've done just what I wanted!

● Look how you've upset your mother by saying that

● I just can't believe you would do this to me

then the chances are you have a problem with asserting yourself. Children love to please others, to gain approval: in some families, they can only do this by toeing a strict party line. In other words, they are not loved and appreciated for themselves, but only to the extent to which they are 'good'. Angry parents create passive children, who fear that any attempt to express individuality will unleash terrible wrath.

The second step in learning to assert yourself is therefore likely to be facing anger or disapproval, and realising that you can – that the world does not end, that you survive, and that the anger of the other person is not your fault.

Something else we seem to learn from babyhood is that things are our fault. Many studies of childhood trauma have shown, for instance, that abused children often feel it's their fault that they are abused (because they're not 'good' enough). Similarly, though less traumatically, the children of parents who separate in acrimonious circumstances or who remain unhappily together often feel that they are somehow to blame for this marital misery.

A point that is made in every assertiveness training course is that as adults we are all responsible for our own feelings and for the way we express them. If I am angry because of something you have done or not done, it is my decision to be angry, and my anger.

There's a moving scene in the film *Good Will Hunting* in which the therapist, Robin Williams, repeats over and over to his anguished client the message 'It's not your fault, it's not your fault, it's not your fault'. If maturity comes as a result of accepting our responsibilities in life and committing ourselves to them, then equally we need to be clear about things which are not our responsibility, and over which we have a needless sense of guilt.

In learning to be assertive, we need to give the right physical messages. In recent years we've all become more aware of body language and what it tells us about other people but we often forget that we ourselves give messages to others by the way we stand, walk and look. Ask close friends for honest feedback about any physical messages you may be unaware of. Some assertiveness training classes use video effectively to let people see – in a supportive environment – how they appear to others.

Points to bear in mind when asserting yourself:

● Always make eye contact with the other person

● Don't smile too much. You want to appear warm, but smiling detracts from what you're saying. (Remember that in the animal world, smiling is a sign of submission intended to defuse threats!)

● Don't fidget with your hands, your jewellery, your hair or anything else; be comfortable and still

● Breathe deeply, so that your voice is steady and audible

● If you tend to use your hands expressively when talking, don't stop doing so - hands can be expressive in asserting oneself but ...

● Don't jab your index finger at people – this is aggressive.

Asserting yourself will consist of verbal skills, too.
Practice these:

● Get straight to the point:
'Jack, I should like the day off on Friday'. Don't start
with a polite preamble or waffle or say *'I – er – oh
sorry I can see you're busy - shall I come back later?'* It's
your boss's job to manage you and the office: you have
a right to his or her time.

● If you have a 'difficult' phone call to make,
prepare beforehand. Write notes for yourself, making
bullet points of the key messages you want to get
across.

● As above, remember to keep breathing deeply.
This not only keeps your voice and your nerves steady
but gives you time to think

● Don't be rushed into things. Practice strategies
like these:
*'Well, that's something to think about, but I'd like a little
time to do so'*; *'Thanks for that, but I need a little time
to think it over'*; *'This has given me lots of ideas, which
I now need to go away and look at again'*.

● When people won't let you have time to think
things through, walk calmly away from them.

● Use prefixes to your remarks such as *'I think'*, *'I
feel'* or *'The way I see it...'* This makes it clear to your
listener that you're speaking for yourself (which is all
you can do).

● Conversely, avoid statements like *'Most people*

think' or *'It's generally felt that'* unless you have the facts to back yourself up. The person you're talking to will just come back to you saying *'Who says so?'* or *'What people?'*

● Express interest in the person you're speaking to by adding phrases such as *'I wonder how you feel about this?'*

If you have promised to get back to someone, get back to them. It is a characteristic of non-assertive people to hope that awkward requests will go away. This is often because of low esteem, which leads the non-assertive person to imagine they are almost invisible to others – or at least not important. In fact, non-assertive people often find themselves arousing anger in other people because they prevaricate and leave things too long. For instance, a person invited to an event he/she does not want to go to may hope that if they leave responding long enough, it will all be forgotten about. The truth is that the host probably thinks they are going and will be all the more annoyed when, at the last minute, they find out the non-assertive person isn't.

As someone who finds assertiveness difficult, I think the answerphone is one of the great inventions of the twentieth century. Telephones intrude and power always seems in the hands (or the voice) of the caller. Answerphones re-empower the person being called, so that they can decide whether or not to speak to the caller, and mull over their response to what is probably being asked of them. But it's a useful practice for assertiveness to get back to your callers promptly, with your response to their request all prepared. A tape full of unanswered messages is stressful and depressing, as well as rude.

If you feel you need some formal help with learning to be assertive, talk to your Human Resources department at work and ask to be sent on a course. If you don't want to do it through work, ask your library for help in locating a course, or contact the Department of Psychology or the Department of Adult Education in the university nearest to you. Someone in either of those departments should be able to help. There are a number of excellent self-help books available too and two of these are listed below. Although written with women in mind, they are equally applicable to men. They contain a wealth of practical ideas and support for the changes you want to make.

Further reading
Anne Dickson, *A Woman in your Own Right.*
Quartet.
Gael Lindenfield, *Assert Yourself.* Thorsons.

Visualisation

Many relaxation classes involve visualisation, but this is something you can do for yourself at home.

At its simplest, visualisation means visualising in your mind scenes or places which bring you peace and refreshment. In more formal visualisation exercises (usually in a class) you may be asked to go on a journey, or perform some simple task. The body must be still and undisturbed, and your mind free to wander, to create, to roam around looking at colours, images, smelling the smells and hearing the sounds of a 'place' inside your head.

You need to find a Me Time – a space in the day when you can ask those you live with to give you time by yourself. You need a room to be comfortable in, preferably away from the rest of the house so that you are not disturbed by doorbells or phones. Unplug the phone and shut your pets outside. Sit in a comfortable chair with your feet on the floor, and remove your shoes.

There are tapes available which can guide you through visualisation exercises. Good health food shops often sell these, and mail order firms advertise in New Age-type magazines or health food magazines.

If you have had a visualisation session in a class,

you may want to remember a similar routine for yourself. Otherwise, just close your eyes, breathe deeply, and feel your own way into a landscape of your choice.

It's important to do this routine slowly. When you begin, spend a few moments consciously calming yourself and focusing on your body: hands relaxed, arms relaxed, legs relaxed, breathing steady and deep. Listen to the sounds around you, smell the smells around you, and spend a moment focusing on your own moods and feelings at that particular moment. How do you feel? Are you happy, tense, worried? A little bored, perhaps? Looking forward to something?

Then gradually widen your focus and step into the place you want to visualise. It may be a room in a house, real or imaginary. It may be a specific place you know – a place where you spent a happy holiday, for instance. It may be your childhood home, or a fictitious place. Imagine you have arrived there – do you walk in through a door? If so, imagine the door and the feelings of the handle under your fingers – is it wood, or brass?

If you are outside and walking to your place, what is the path like? Are you coming round a bend on a hillside, or walking along a beach? If you have bare feet, what can you feel beneath your feet – soft

earth, or sand, or leaves in a wood? What sounds
can you hear – waves tumbling on a shore, birds
calling in the trees, perhaps a wood pigeon? Are
you in some exotic place where you can hear the
cry of exotic birds and wild animals, or in a British
wood listening to blackbirds? What are the scents
in this place – if you're in a room, perhaps you can
smell beeswax from the furniture polish, or flowers,
or wood burning in the grate? If outside, perhaps
you can smell herbs, or roses? (Not all the things
you visualise have to be this perfect – a friend of
mine always visualises her childhood home on a
farm, and would not be happy unless she could
smell wet dogs and pig manure!)

Focus on every detail of the place you are in.
Then imagine yourself there. What are you doing?
Perhaps you want to rest for a moment with the sun
on your face. If you are in a room, perhaps you
want to sit for a while, warming your hands against
the fire. Spend a while in that place. Just be there,
and rest.

Often this is a good moment to repeat some
affirmations to yourself (see below).

Gradually, ease your consciousness back to the
present moment. Walk away from the place.
Perhaps you close the door quietly, perhaps you
take the path back up the hill from the beach.

Slowly, slowly, become aware of your own body here again, in this room, in your house, now, today. Focus on your breathing.

Open your eyes.

Wait for a few moments before you leave this room and go off to do other things.

A visualisation can last as long as you wish, though it's hard to feel truly rested if you have less than ten minutes to spare. But even if you only have ten minutes every day to give yourself this Me Time, the rewards can be great.

Affirmation

This can also be described as auto-suggestion or self-instruction. Basically, it means repeating positive things to yourself about yourself, until you believe them. This self-belief then boosts confidence and enhances self-esteem so that a virtuous circle is created.

The words and phrases used in affirmations are carefully selected: after all, the intention is that they will come to be true. It's a technique derived from many Eastern religions such as Buddhism, where a significant part of religious practice consists of the repetitions of chants or mantras - the words have meaning, but the repetition itself focuses the mind, calms the body and induces a sense of wellbeing.

Affirmations, as their name implies, must be positive: '*I think I should like to have the job advertised in the paper although I don't think I'm good enough*' is not an affirmation.

In that particular circumstance, a better choice of words would be: '*I know that I am ready to move on and I am confident that an opportunity awaits me*'.

Affirmations are fine as part of a wider programme to generate self-confidence and self-esteem, in which phrases such as the following might be selected: '*I am worthy of love and respect, and I offer these gifts back to those around me'. 'I respect and cherish the child within me, and within all other people'. 'I feel love and strength, and radiate these to the world'.*

Another use for affirmations is when you want to defuse negative thoughts or emotions such as anger or jealousy.

After an acrimonious personal break-up, for instance, an affirmation may help the healing process:

'I gave love freely, and will do so again. Now it is time to move on without bitterness or jealousy, because I am worthy of love and respect'.

Buddhist chanting has, of course, gained wide publicity through adherents such as Tina Turner, who has said that regular chanting helped her turn her life around in a positive way after her break-up with Ike. Many Buddhist centres now offer instruction, irrespective of whether the individual is a follower of Buddhism or not.

Mindfulness

There is another useful mental technique to be borrowed from Eastern religions. In Buddhism this is called 'mindfulness'.

Most of the time, during the day, our minds wander all over the place – into the past, the future, the events of yesterday, what we're going to have for supper, our plans for the weekend. Like grazing animals, our minds go everywhere. Seldom do they focus simply on the here and now.

Yet the present moment is all that we ever truly have. The past is gone; we cannot know the future. In worrying and wondering, we fritter away the time that we have this instant. We are not focusing on the reality of now.

The more focused we are, the more effectively we work and play and interact with other people.

The technique of mindfulness is simply to tether your mind and bring it gently back to the now whenever it wanders. Be watchful and careful of each moment of your life. As you clean your teeth, as you walk to the bus stop, as you eat or work and talk with friends, be here now.

When you catch your mind skipping away to a past or future date, gently guide it back to what you are purposefully and calmly doing right at this moment. It is all that you truly have.

Say to yourself: *be of the moment.*

Pre-Menstrual Syndrome (PMS)

It would be impossible to write a book about stress and not mention pre-menstrual syndrome (also called pre-menstrual tension, although few women experience just the one single symptom).

PMS affects thousands of women in a variety of ways, and inevitably it also affects their partners, families and colleagues. Unless it is very mild, it is almost impossible to suffer PMS and not have other people notice.

Until recent years, few doctors believed there was such a condition. Mood swings and erratic behaviour were put down to lack of self-control, or just being a hysterical female. (The word hysteria comes from the same root as the word for uterus or womb). Since the pioneering work of Dr Katharina Dalton in the 1950s, who was the first to recognise that it was a hormonal imbalance and to treat her patients with progesterone, the medical profession has slowly come to recognise PMS as a definable condition, and many respected practitioners now work exclusively in this field.

There is still no one single answer as to what causes PMS, though most agree that hormonal imbalance lies at the heart of it and there is disagreement as to whether treatment with hormones (such as progesterone or synthetic replacements) is the best remedy. There is no disagreement, however, as to the symptoms:

Physical – water retention, bloating, swollen and tender breasts, backache.

Emotional – mood swings, irritability, weepiness, depression, uncontrollable or 'irrational' rage.

Women have committed suicide and murder while suffering from PMS. The damage done to families, careers and relationships is incalculable. The ultimate cure – hysterectomy – is drastic and many women point out angrily that this is a typically male response: they would not be so quick to cut off bits of themselves just because it was troublesome. Moreover, hysterectomy is a major operation with all the dangers and possible side effects that that entails. Many women, however, who have suffered a lifetime of PMS, vouch for the effectiveness and desirability of this solution, and the very fact that they are willing to go through with the operation demonstrates the strength of their feelings about PMS.

Most doctors still prescribe hormonal treatments for PMS; a few are now also turning to the anti-depressant drug, Prozac, which has had reported successes in treating it. Prozac belongs to a group of drugs called Selective Serotonin

Reuptake Inhibitors (SSRIs). Women with PMS have been shown to have lower levels of serotonin in their blood, and when brain serotonin levels are boosted using one of these drugs, symptoms improve.

Many women will, however, be uneasy at the thought of taking a drug for the rest of their reproductive lives; others will have milder symptoms and not need to resort to such measures.

There are a number of natural remedies and complementary therapies that have benefited PMS sufferers, and a summary of self-help recommendations is given below.

- Vitamin B6 and Evening Primrose oil

- Homeopathic remedies such as sepia, pulsatilla

- Avoid coffee, tea and alcohol when pre-menstrual – these stimulate the system in ways you do not need, while alcohol is a mood enhancer and PMS moods do not need enhancing

- Eat six small meals of high-carbohydrate, low-sugar foods, such as pasta or a baked potato, throughout the day. Do not get hungry and allow your blood sugar to fall

- Exercise is beneficial especially swimming, or walking and running in the fresh air

- Reflexology

- Yoga

It is also worth pointing out that many women feel that PMS is a natural response to the circumstances of women's lives in a male-dominated world. With the heightened awareness and sensitivity that PMS brings, they feel angry and suffocated and unable to express their real feelings appropriately. Instead of 'damping down' the symptoms with drugs or surgery, women should study assertiveness and learn to express themselves fully and without fear.

The National Association for Pre-menstrual Syndrome has a Helpline on 01732 760012 and their Website is www.pms.org.uk

HELP FROM OTHER PEOPLE

In some circles, bringing words like 'therapy' or 'counselling' into a conversation can still earn sideways glances or a sudden silence. This is unfortunate. We've come a long way from the stereotypical image of Woody Allen spending years on a couch talking to his analyst about his 'neuroses'. For a start, no psychotherapist would expect a client to lie down and thus feel vulnerable or disempowered – unless the client wanted to. Most sessions take place face to face, sitting comfortably.

Many people now see counsellors or therapists on a regular basis – for a short or a long period of time – not because they are mentally ill or depressed or even because they have a specific problem they want to solve, but because they appreciate the many and varied benefits they receive from 'the talking therapy'.

For the avoidance of doubt, let's make a distinction straight away between psychiatrists who receive referrals from the medical profession and who are 'doctors of the mind' treating recognised illnesses, and psychotherapists or counsellors (the terms are often used interchangeably) who are not medically qualified and who offer different types of therapy to their clients. There may often be an overlap. For instance, people with mild forms of an eating disorder may voluntarily choose to see a counsellor in an informal setting. But someone who is seriously ill with anorexia is more likely to be treated in a hospital setting and work with a psychiatrist.

Another distinction is that psychiatrists, because they are medically trained, will tend to follow a 'medical model' of practice. That is: I am the doctor, you are the patient, you are ill, I will tell you what to do, I am in charge of your condition (and because of the nature of many mental illnesses, this may be entirely right and necessary). Generally speaking, psychotherapy follows another path: I am a therapist, you are my client, I will listen with empathy to what you have to say, I cannot and will not tell you what to do, I will share your journey of discovery and recovery with you, walking by your side.

Just as you don't have to have a specific medical condition to feel the benefits of having a massage or studying Alexander Technique, you don't need to have a specific psychological trauma to want to see a psychotherapist. In fact, nobody can qualify as a psychotherapist until they have been through the process themselves as a client. Therapy is a healthy thing to do, a way of being serious about your psychic health just as taking regular exercise or learning a relaxation technique are ways of being serious about your physical health.

Which therapist?

There are many different schools of psychotherapy and many different styles of counselling. Practitioners are variously trained. Some will have degrees and diplomas in psychology or psychotherapy; voluntary organisations like Relate, for instance, may employ volunteers with no formal qualifications who have undergone their own training course.

Many therapists will advertise themselves as following a particular school of psychotherapy such as gestalt. Others will describe themselves as using an eclectic approach – that is, having taken little bits from many other philosophies and blended them together into a personal approach.

It is also important to distinguish between 'general' psychotherapists whose primary concern is the individual, and organisations that exist to offer counselling in specific areas. These include Relate, which was founded to work with marital and relationship problems, and Cruse, which offers bereavement counselling, as well as many of the organisations offering support to people who are HIV positive or ill with AIDS. In this section, I am principally concerned with 'general' psychotherapy and counselling.

At the time of writing, the legal situation is that

there is nothing to stop anyone putting up a brass plaque and calling themselves a therapist. The profession is voluntarily regulated, and this is something that most therapists themselves want to see changed. That's why it's important to check the validity of the therapist you are seeing, and why a good starting point may well be the British Association for Counselling (address at the end of the book).

It's important that you trust your therapist and feel you can work comfortably with this person.

Below, I outline the basics of some of the main types of psychotherapy. There are others. Sometimes local centres of counselling or psychotherapy offer day or weekend courses as introductions to gestalt or TA or cognitive behavioural therapy, and it's worth looking out for these – your library or a big health food store or 'alternative' cafe are usually useful sources of information. If you live in an area that has its own listings magazine (such as *Time Out* in London or *The List* in Scotland) it's worth checking there too.

It goes without saying that the notes I make below about some of the main schools of psychotherapy are just that – brief sketches. They barely touch the surface of these areas, which are in themselves rich, varied and complex, and individually worth many years of study. If you feel that one or more of these approaches might suit you, I'd suggest you look for further reading on the subject and contact local therapists who work in this way.

Client-centred counselling

The person- (or client-) centred approach may also
be called a humanistic approach to counselling,
and some of the founding fathers of this movement
include Gerard Egan, Eugene Heimler and Viktor
Frankl. The main name you will hear, though, is
the American Carl Rogers (1902-1987) who wrote
many books about his approach to counselling in
which he emphasises that three core conditions
must be present in the therapist: empathy,
genuineness and non-possessive warmth.

In client-centred counselling, no advice is given:
the therapist is non-directional. You will never
hear your therapist say *'you should'* or *'you ought'*.
The therapist will avoid directly expressing his or
her opinion – what he will do instead is reflect back
to you his impressions of what you are feeling. For
instance, the therapist may listen to you talking
about an issue that concerns you greatly and
comment *'I can sense that this causes you a lot of
pain'*.

Carl Rogers believed that each person already
has the resources within to heal his or her own self.
The client knows what is best: she may have lost
touch with her own inner voice and feel unable to
trust her own instincts, but the trust at the heart of
client-centred therapy is that by purposeful talking

with a counsellor, the client can recover the ability to listen to herself and direct her own life. The counsellor is a facilitator: his or her own personality should not intrude.

In client-centred counselling, you will find the word 'problems' replaced by the word 'issues'. This is significant, and especially perhaps for clients who seek help with stress-related issues. The reason is that the word problems may carry connotations of blame, and ultimately of resolution of the problem as a final solution. In other words, if A is my problem, and I can find a solution for A, then there will be no more problems. In fact, the 'problem' may re-occur in a different form because it is the result of an attitude or an unexpressed need on the part of the client; issues are the fabric of life. They do not have to necessarily be solved but lived with, understood and accommodated.

Eugene Heimler (1922–1991) used the experience of his own terrible suffering in Auschwitz to develop what he termed 'connective counselling'. In a wonderful phrase, he referred to the 'the pearl inside each of us' and felt that all life was a search to find meaning. In Auschwitz, he observed that some people gave up the struggle to live and died because they had lost all sense of meaning. In the search for meaning, Heimler said

that we should connect our past with our present –
present events have their roots in our past and only
by integrating the two can we find wholeness.

A technique of value here is called the 'Slice of
Life'. The client thinks of a situation in the last 24
hours which has triggered pain or strong emotion
(such as feelings of stress). She is then invited to
link the feeling engendered by that emotion with
an event or happening in the deep past – usually in
early childhood.

Gestalt therapy

The founder of gestalt, Fritz Perls (1893–1970) trained in Freudian psychoanalysis but later described psychoanalysis as 'crap'. Born in a Jewish ghetto in Berlin, he left Germany with the rise of Nazism and went to live in South Africa, leaving only when apartheid was introduced. He died in California.

The word gestalt itself is a German word meaning 'whole' or 'pattern' or 'configuration', and so the gestalt process is a holistic process – that is, the mind, body and senses are all seen as part of the same unity, not as separate elements.

Gestalt is described as an 'actualising' approach. That means, the aim is to become who you are. Perls felt that the individual beings we were born to be become clouded and muddled by struggling in society to be what others want us to be. He wrote: 'A rose is not intent to actualise itself as a kangaroo... In nature, except for the human being, constitution, and healthiness, potential, growth, is all one unified something... We [humans] find ourselves on the one hand as individuals who want to actualise themselves; we find ourselves also embedded in a society, and this society makes demands on us different from the individual demands. So there is a basic clash'.

Gestalt seeks to resolve this clash. The aim of gestalt therapy may be simply defined as 'awareness'. Awareness itself is therapeutic; when the mind is cluttered with needs which are not met or feelings which are not accepted it is said to be blocked with 'unfinished business', and it is the aim of gestalt – through facilitating awareness – to 'unblock' the individual and finish the business.

How then does it work in practical terms?
Gestalt is a 'quick' form of therapy: clients are usually only asked to commit themselves to a short number of sessions (often as few as four or six) whereas other types of counselling may be open-ended, but usually with a minimum commitment of several months. Gestalt often takes place in group sessions, and certain ground rules (or 'adjustments') are laid down for the group which help the individual adjust to the idea of 'taking responsibility for my own self' (which is a key gestalt building block). These adjustments include:

In therapy, the client is not to speak about someone but rather to them – even if that person is not present, you should speak directly to them. Thus if you are talking to the therapist about your mother, you should address your remarks as if your mother were sitting opposite you. The idea behind this is that it encourages openness and responsibility but that we should also direct remarks and behaviour where they belong. (See the two-chair process, below).

Make statements not questions. In gestalt, clients are encouraged to say *'I think that...'* or *'I want to...'* rather than *'Do you think I should?'* or *'Would it be a good idea if I...?'* This means you are asserting yourself and speaking for your own needs rather than seeking the approval of other people.

Say *'I'* not *'one'* or *'people'*. Gestalt encourages individual responsibility. Thus you can only really say *'I want to do this'* or *'I feel that this is right'*. Using expressions like *'one does not always want to do this'* or *'most people would think...'* dilutes your individuality.

Change the passive to the active. For example, instead of saying *'My boss upset me by saying that'* you should say: *'I allowed myself to become upset by what my boss said to me'*. The change in emphasis is clear: I take responsibility for the way I feel. People do not make me do things, I choose to do them.

In gestalt therapy, the client is encouraged to set up a dialogue or a series of dialogues with other parts of his own personality. As we saw above, Perls felt that conflict arose from who we want to be and really are and who others think we are or ought to be. A technique of gestalt is to encourage a dialogue between these two parts and this is sometimes done by asking the client to use two chairs. When he sits in one chair, he is (for example) the person he really wants to be; when he expresses the views of the 'other', he must move to the other chair. In this very graphic way, the client comes to a literal awareness of the parts that make up the whole. This technique can also be used when, in therapy, we need to place feelings where they really belong.

In other words, if a client considers himself an 'angry' person whose anger tends to spill out generally into all areas of his life, but he can recognise that that anger actually comes from his relationship with his father, then in the two-chair scenario he can 'be' both his childhood self and his father, and conduct a dialogue with his father, directing his anger, fully and focusedly, where it has always belonged.

Further reading
Frederick S Perls, *Gestalt Therapy.* Souvenir Press.
Gaie Houston, *The Red Book of Gestalt.* Rochester.
Muriel Schiffman, *Gestalt Self Therapy.* Wingbow.
Richard G Abell, *Own your own Life.* Bantam.

Transactional analysis (TA)

TA is a school of psychotherapy which, as its name implies, seeks to analyse the transactions of our lives: in other words, we don't exist in isolation but as part of a network of relationships – with family, with partner, with colleagues and of course with our own selves. If we understand the nature of these various transactions and the way we handle them, we have a better understanding of ourselves.

The foundation stone of TA is the ego-state theory of personality. This means, that at any time I may be expressing my personality from one of three ego-states within myself. Whichever ego state I am in will define how I behave.

These three states are:

- Parent
- Adult
- Child

For instance, in comforting a friend and trying to be supportive, I could be acting from my Parent ego state: nurturing and loving. If I have to make a financial decision, I am probably acting from the Adult ego state, which sifts information and evaluates it and reaches conclusions based on evidence. Among friends or with family at home, I

might be acting from Child, which is usually
defined as playful and spontaneous.

Note that all the terms used in TA have a very
specific meaning within TA. To be in a 'Child ego
state' does not (necessarily) mean that you are
being childish or even childlike. This use of
everyday terms but with a new, deeper meaning is
often quite baffling to those unfamiliar with TA.

Each ego state has positive and negative
attributes. Our inner Parent, for example, may be a
Nurturing Parent ('there, there, it'll be all right') or
a Controlling Parent ('don't do that'). Our inner
Child may be a Free Child (inquisitive, impulsive,
adventurous) or an Adapted Child (trained and
restrained) – as real children often become when
they have very controlling parents.

Adult seeks to bring balance and harmony:
Adult is the voice of reason. Adult is a filter: the
Parent and Child ego states have their roots in the
past, with how your real parents were and how you
were as a real child, but Adult is in the here and
now, and concerned with today's reality. So for
example if my Adapted Child inner voice says to
me 'This is scary, I'll fail, better not do that' my
Adult can step in and respond with: 'There's no
evidence that you'll fail. Given the situation and
what I know of the conditions, I think this is a

sensible course of action'.

We can move between these ego states all the time and they are utterly flexible – unless, that is, there is a blockage somewhere (see below). And they are all needed. Controlling Parent, for example, might seem like a repressive force; but in fact it's Controlling Parent who tells you not to touch bare wires, and to look carefully before crossing the road.

A TA therapist will spend some time outlining this theory and explaining the characteristics of the different ego states. The reason, quite simply, is that we can see where we're coming from. Although I might like to think I spend a lot of my time acting from Adult – calm, rational, sensible – my time in TA therapy taught me to see just how much of the time I spend in Adapted Child, trying to please, trying to 'be good'.

When one ego state is dominant most of the time, or when movement to another ego state is blocked for some reason, there is an imbalance. A healthy personality may be defined as one in which the individual moves happily between all five go states in an appropriate way, as the circumstances demand. In some personal relationships, for instance, one partner may spend most of the time acting from Controlling Parent and the other partner from Adapted Child. All is 'well' until Adapted Child wants to move into Adult, say – the transaction then becomes crossed or blocked. What TA therapy seeks to do is unblock our free access to the component parts of our personality and give us choice over which state to be in. It is a simple, straightforward and very direct way of understanding our personality and therefore our behaviour.

My outline is a gross simplification, however, and I do urge the interested reader to read a fuller account of what TA is and what it can do. Recommended books are listed below and they in turn contain fuller reading lists.

Many other ideas underpin this basic structure of TA and I only have room to mention a few very briefly here, because they have particular relevance to stress.

Strokes

We need to be 'stroked' – literally. Recent studies in Romanian orphanages have shown that abandoned babies die from a lack of physical contact: their spines fail to develop, and their little bodies shrivel and perish. Babies cannot develop normally if deprived of the touch of hands and the warmth of a maternal, or proxy maternal, body.

Dogs and cats lick their puppies and kittens constantly: they are not just grooming them and bonding with them, they are actually stimulating appetite by licking and so helping their offspring to grow.

As babies, we needed the physical touch of our mothers but as adults we need strokes too: we need friends, family and colleagues to validate our worth. Here are some examples of things we might say which 'stroke' other people in a positive way.

- *I love you*
- *Gosh, this is a great casserole*
- *I could not have done this without you*
- *These sales figures are just what I wanted*

Saying 'thank you' as you get off a bus is stroking the driver: you are acknowledging his existence and validating him, that is, acknowledging that he is a separate and important individual.

Strokes can be negative, too, and we all have experience of these:

- *Why do you always have to wear that ghastly coat?*
- *What kind of sales figures do you call these, Smith?*
- *Is that the best you can do?*

- *I hate you*
- *Leave me alone*
- *Bloody kids, get off my garden*

We can also reject positive strokes. If someone says 'you look wonderful' and you respond with 'you need your eyes testing, my hair looks awful' this is a mild form of rejecting a positive stroke; the exchange 'I love you' 'No you don't' is a very emphatic rejection of a stroke.

Discounting leads on from negative stroking, for discounting means ignoring or devaluing a person or an experience. The parent who neglects or ignores their child (even if only temporarily) is discounting them. The wife who says loudly in a restaurant: 'My husband won't have the Pavlova. He's got a weak stomach and rich puddings keep him up all night' is discounting: talking about a real, present being in the third person, depriving them of their own individuality and responsibility for themselves.

Scripts and games
TA says that individuals in whom the Adult is not developed, people who do not function as autonomous beings, follow a 'script' of life and play

'games', and a common tool in TA therapy is to encourage the client to examine their own life for traces of script and game-playing. In most of us, it's unavoidable. Various fun devices (such as encouraging people to think of a slogan to put on a T-shirt which encapsulates their life position, or write their own epitaphs) have a serious goal: to help us spot repetitive patterns of behaviour (scripts).

Eric Berne, the founder of TA, identified numerous games in his book *Games People Play*. Many of us will have played at least one of them at some time or another. The point of a game is that it brings a pay-off to those who play it: both parties gain something (even if it's negative, usually because it's negative) and a game cannot be played if one party is aware that it is a game, and withdraws from it.

Let's take one extreme example to illustrate this. A man is alcoholic. There will be a trigger point – a bad day at work, a nagging letter from the bank, his parking space taken by someone else – and he will go on a drinking spree. This leads to a row at home with his wife, whom he abuses verbally and physically. He is then overcome by remorse, breaks down, begs for forgiveness, promises to reform. His wife forgives him, and peace is restored. And then the whole game can begin all over again.

What is the pay-off here? On the surface, it appears such a distressing situation for all concerned. But this is the important point about games: they cause such havoc and unhappiness, but for the players, this is the only way to get in touch with their deepest reality.

It is a basic theory of TA that our deepest reality (the emotional feelings with which we feel most comfortable and at home) may in fact be negative and unhappy emotions. This is because this is the earliest reality we lived with, as a child. As babies and children we don't know and can't use words; we only know feelings. And if the only feelings we know are bad ones, then, subconsciously, that's what we try to get back to.

In the story above, the man learned as a child to feel 'comfortable' with his own self-hatred: as an adult, abusing himself through drink followed by bad behaviour towards another person is a sure way of achieving regular 'fixes' of self-hatred. A great part of the game is his conviction that he is not responsible for his drinking: other people make him do it.

As for the woman, it's likely given the circumstances that she had a discounting father (that is, one who ignored her) who created around her an atmosphere of instability and upset. In subsequent relationships, she may say that she's looking for a caring, loving man 'not at all like her father' but in fact she is only 'comfortable' (that is, she only feels quite literally 'at home') in an environment which exactly replicates the emotional chaos of her childhood.

What, you may well ask, has all this got to do with stress?

I think people who admit to living with high levels of stress could be helped by looking at the following issues.

● Responsibility. Nobody makes you stressed, you allow yourself to become stressed. This is not a 'fault' and indeed in the circumstances may be perfectly understandable - but accept your stress as your responsibility, something that is yours, not other people's.

● If you are game playing, or among people who play games as a (probably subconscious) way of manipulating others, you will feel very stressed. If you can spot repetitive patters of negative behaviour in those around you – in which you are involved – which lead to a crisis and a pay-off before they start up all over again, then you have the chance of withdrawing yourself from such negative activity.

● If stress is a regular part of your life, and comes from feelings within yourself, then the script of your

life – a script developed in your earliest childhood –
can be changed.

● You are not the only one acting from one of the
five ego states: so is everyone else. Thus when your
boss gives you a negative stroke by saying 'Haven't
you finished yet?' and your automatic reaction is to
feel 'I've failed', analysing the situation in TA terms
and realising that you have gone straight into blame-
taking Adapted Child (while the boss obviously
wishes to be Controlling Parent) brings perspective
and balance to a stressful situation and shows you
how to resolve it – by choosing to move into Adult
and handling it that way ('No, actually I didn't have
enough time').

The key to changing any area of your life or your
behaviour is first of all awareness. Awareness of
what the patterns are, of what – in therapy speak –
the issues are. Therapy can help to uncover your
awareness and in so doing give you the support you
need while change takes place.

Further reading
Ian Stewart and Vann Joines, *TA Today*. Lifespace.
Muriel James and Dorothy Jongeward, *Born to Win*.
Addison Wesley.
Thomas A. Harris, *I'm OK, You're OK*. Arrow.
Eric Berne, *Games People Play*. Penguin.

Cognitive therapy

Cognitive behaviour therapy has its origins with the Russian scientist Pavlov and his experiments with dogs. A bell rings, food is brought to a group of dogs, the dogs see the food and begin to salivate in anticipation, and they are fed. Eventually, the dogs begin to salivate when the bell is rung - they know what to expect next.

This, Pavlov argued, is also applicable to humans: behaviour is learned from experience. At the heart of cognitive therapy lies the belief that what is learned can also be unlearned if it proves not to be helpful to us.

There's an old saying 'success breeds success' and recent studies among businessmen have shown that a positive outlook is linked with success. If you believe you will succeed, you are more likely to do so than the person with a negative outlook. Professor Jeffrey Gray of the Institute of Psychiatry analysed the acceptance speeches by American presidential candidates, and found that in 17 out of 20 elections, the candidate who won used the greater number of optimistic phrases.

'Optimism' in this context has a special meaning. Professor Gray says that there are three aspects to the explanations we give for what happens: these are internal, stable and pervasive.

Imagine this conversation, for instance. A man is late for a business meeting and his boss asks him why. 'My plane was delayed by fog', he replies calmly. To analyse this reply using the three aspects-

Internal	He is not blaming himself for being late; external circumstances were to blame and there was nothing he could do about it
Stable	The fog is not permanent; he won't be late next time and he wasn't late last time
Pervasive	Delayed by fog is one minor incident and it doesn't colour his whole career: he is not a less valuable or experienced worker

The 'pessimist', on the other hand, would internalise and agonise over the whole situation, taking blame for the fog, the late arrival of the plane, his boss's anger, and everything else upon himself.

Cognitive therapy works in a limited number of sessions (usually no more than 15 and often about ten) to help people observe themselves being negative or pessimistic, and to change their behaviour. When clients are encouraged to be positive and optimistic, this does not mean they should be unrealistically so: it's simply that when the facts of the situation are observed, negative attitudes often don't 'stand up in court'.

Many forms of therapy begin with the past and in delving into their childhoods clients may be overwhelmed by emotion. Cognitive therapy focuses more on thinking, and on the here and now.

Many therapists work by asking the clients to keep a series of charts describing real situations and the feelings they had or have about them which are then discussed during sessions. An example of such a chart might go like this:

Feeling: *I'm utterly depressed and wretched and useless. I don't want to go on.* Situation: *My boyfriend has just dumped me and is going out with someone else.*

Thought: *I hate myself, I'm worthless, if I was as good as his new girlfriend he wouldn't have dumped me, I'm not as good as she is*

Alternative thought: *I am not worth nothing just because a relationship ends and leaves me in pain. I'm feeling pain because I'm a real, human person who can be hurt. My boyfriend's behaviour is his responsibility, I don't have to dwell on it and get bitter, I have my own life to get on with – a life that was whole before I met him and will be so again soon.*

Outcome: The client's negative thoughts had

followed her ex-boyfriend out of the door; she had sent her own sense of selfhood after him instead of keeping it firmly focused upon herself.

Cognitive therapy is a useful tool for living with, and can be of especial benefit to those who feel themselves to be under tremendous amounts of stress.

If the causes of stress can be looked at individually in this manner, and optimistic responses put in place of more negative ones, stress can lift. For example:

Feeling: *I'm useless and worthless, I don't deserve to have a job, this whole situation's gone pear-shaped*

Situation: *I lost that important contract with Bloggs and Bloggs*

Thought: *I'll get the sack, I'll never get a job again*

Alternative thought: *Bloggs and Bloggs have been difficult customers for years and it's been obvious to all of us that our product is not quite right for them. We have other customers who are very happy with the service I give them, and my record is good. I've learned something from this experience, and I'm going to apply that when I deal with the new clients I'm going to go out and get.*

Outcome: *This person was taking responsibility that did not belong to him. He was seeing the defection of Bloggs and Bloggs as a personal failure, when the most likely reason is that there were a number of other commercial factors behind their decision.*

It's important to realise that cognitive therapy is not about letting individuals off the hook by saying 'it's not my fault'. If something is most definitely my 'fault', then I need to take responsibility for it, own up, and learn from the experience. But many of us feel that everything is our fault, and we enter a spiral of negativism when something goes wrong, believing that if one thing goes wrong, it's inevitable that everything else will. Experience shows that it does not.

Part 3
COPING FROM THE OUTSIDE

This final section looks at ways of handling stress from the outside: by looking after our bodies, our health, our physical wellbeing.

Most of the therapies I discuss briefly cost money. That immediately puts them beyond the reach of many people.

But there are a number of other strategies for coping, which cost nothing or comparatively little, and can be just as effective. The American writer Thoreau once wrote: 'Beware of all enterprises that require new clothes'. If the cost of gaining health or reducing stress in your life is an overdraft's worth of new clothes or equipment, forget it. A brisk walk in the fresh air is just as good for you.

YOUR HEALTH

Most of life's challenges can be met a whole lot better if you are in good physical health. Think of a difficult day at work with (a) a streaming head cold or (b) feeling fit on a sunny bright day and you will see what I mean. The exuberance of small children playing can seem like a scenario from hell if you are tired, or have flu, or are just plain below par.

I am not talking about the peak fitness of an athlete – achieving that state can bring its own stresses.

In dealing with stress in your life, resolve now to look after your health and seek to improve it. Health brings its own beauty and a sense of genuine wellbeing is worth millions.

Unoriginally, let's look at the achievement of health as comprising two strands: diet and exercise. It's possible to achieve one without the other. There are plenty of physically fit people – the teenage rugby player comes to mind – who live on a diet of chips and beer. There are lots of people who are very careful about their diet but would rather die than walk from the car to the pavement (though not many, I suspect). But it's now widely accepted that optimum health is achieved by paying attention to both.

The 'D' word

Hands up if you don't yawn when you read the word diet. It must be the second most over-used four-letter word in recent years.

The diet industry – that is, the industry that extracts millions of pounds sterling from people every year with the promise of removing pounds of flab from their bodies – is worth billions. Diet books are successful largely because they don't work. We come back for more because we believe that this time, this time, it will be okay and we will get thin and everything will be hunky dory.

Nowadays, we think of 'diet' almost exclusively in terms of trying to lose weight. The idea of diet as being simply 'what you eat' has been swallowed up (if you'll excuse the pun) in that concept. The idea of diet as being 'eating to be healthy' or (heaven forbid) 'eating for pleasure' is far outweighed, literally, by the notion that we must all of us be very slim. This obsession with thinness has led to the curious state of affairs that in an affluent culture many people are indeed thin to the point where their health has been jeopardised.

Eating disorders such as anorexia and bulimia are now widespread, and many books have been written about them. Both often start simply as a diet that goes wrong. A person thinks 'If only I lost a stone, everything would be okay'. She (it is usually a she, though boys and men are increasingly affected) loses 14lbs, but everything is not all right. In the sad hope that another stone will do the trick, the person goes on dieting, and on and on, until the illness itself takes over, distorting all rational sense of body shape or image.

It should be pointed out that both illnesses are often responses to stress. Anorexia is a way of achieving control in a seemingly helpless situation: the anorectic feels she can control nothing about her life, but in a chaotic world, she can control her diet, can force her own body to submit.

Similarly, the bulimic seeks comfort in food as a temporary means of alleviating great burdens of stress and unhappiness. Once the food has been ingested, guilt and a fear of gaining weight take over, and they force themselves to vomit the get rid of it. Both conditions are chronic and the cause of immense distress and suffering: if you yourself are suffering, or feel you are vulnerable, seek help now. You are not alone, and your pain is great.

If you are overweight, and that in itself is making you feel stressed and unhappy, you will want to find a way of resolving that situation. Most diet advice can be summed up in a sentence: eat less; avoid too much sugar and starch; take exercise. There is so much information available on dieting that there cannot be a person on the planet who does not realise that apples are better than cream buns, and a plain baked potato better than chips. If you seriously want to lose weight, you will find a whole rack of magazines and shelves of books to tell you how.

But losing weight is as much about attitude and readiness as replacing chips with crispbread. What our society calls excess weight may in fact be fulfilling a function for you: it's easier to blame the weight for your personal problems than to face the problems themselves. This is not to accuse overweight people of being unable to face up to life: on the contrary, they have often struggled very hard with life's problems, and been temporarily defeated. Overweight people usually trash themselves so much; they don't need other people to do it for them.

What I am saying is that carrying too much weight – if and only if it is a cause of anguish for that person – has a psychological element to it, and understanding that is more important than understanding the relative calorie values of a cappuccino or an espresso. The phrase 'comfort eating' has a meaning for many people and when you need comfort and a cream bun is what you want, have it. Without the guilt topping.

Diets and diet books have a very judgmental stance, and transfer this to the dieters. The way they talk about 'good' and 'bad' in terms of food. Salads are 'good', chocolate is 'bad'. It's only a small step from this kind of meaningless tosh (if all you eat is one Mars Bar a day you will be thin; if all you eat are loads of oily salads your weight is not likely to alter by one ounce) to the state of mind whereby the poor dieter, worn out by the bleak boredom of a life on salads, eats one Mars Bar and thereby feels herself to be 'bad'.

The healthy diet

Scarcely a week passes without more newspaper articles about wonder foods and the exact composition of the healthiest diet. One week dairy foods are in, the next they're out. Because Japanese people have a low incidence of cardiovascular disease and they eat lots of fish, we are encouraged to eat fish. The same low incidence of heart disease is found among Mediterranean people, and they eat lots of olive oil and butter plays no part in their diet. And so on.

Based on information currently available, the following would seem to be good advice for a diet that is healthy and promotes that indefinable sense of wellbeing:

● Throw out your frying pan. Grill meat and fish, or bake it in the oven. If you need convincing, grill a lamb chop and then look at the fat left at the bottom of the grill pan. When you fry your chop that – plus the fat you fry in – is going into your body; blocking up your arteries and not doing much for the size of your bum either

● Try to cut down on hard-core red meats like beef and lamb and go for chicken and fish instead.

● Try to include as much organic/free range food in your diet as possible.

● Avoid sugar where you can. Certainly learn to

drink tea and coffee without it – and don't use artificial sweeteners instead. Artificial sweeteners are full of the direst gunk – you're better off with sugar frankly.

● While we're bashing artificial sweeteners over the head, remember that fizzy drinks are full of them. Try switching to carbonated or plain water instead or natural fruit juices. People with a professional interest in a clear and healthy complexion mutter '1.5 litres of water' a day as if it were a mantra. Ideal advice, but remember two things: you must always be near a reliable loo; and bottled water is expensive - but unless you live in London or some huge urban area, tap water in the UK is actually okay. Not sexy, maybe, but okay for you and much better than orange fizzy stuff in a can.

● A beautiful 68-year-old model who recently featured in Marks and Spencer ads claimed that drinking lots and lots of water was her one beauty secret.

● Coffee and tea should be drunk sparingly and drink only the best. If the only way you can stop wearing out the carpet to the coffee machine at work is to go cold turkey, do it. You will have a crippling headache and a furry mouth when you give up coffee. That proves you're addicted to a toxic substance.

● And, yes, you guessed it: lots of vegetables (preferably steamed or stir-fried), lots of fresh fruit, lots of salads smothered in lovely virgin olive oil

- No food is good for you if you eat too much of it.
- No food is bad for you if you just have a little.

The scales in your bathroom can tell you nothing useful. Every diet book and magazine contains 'ideal weights' per height and many people strive energetically to reach them. What really matters, however, is how you feel inside yourself and how you look to yourself.

Exercise

Regular exercise, as we all know, benefits the body. The 1980s and 1990s witnessed an absolute boom in gyms, exercise classes, fitness magazines, fun runs and 'new' exercise regimes such as Pilates; thousands of us poured money into these in the hope of achieving a firm, toned, fit body.

But exercise also benefits the mind, and especially the stressed mind.

If you take only one thing away with you from this book, please let it be that making room in your life for regular exercise is the best thing you can do in your strategy for managing stress.

Stress is a state of high energy, and not using or directing that energy leaves you edgy and frustrated. Exercise will channel that energy and use it, leaving you pleasantly tired and satisfied.

When we exercise, chemicals called endorphins are released into the brain. These endorphins are the body's natural form of morphine. Like that other drug, endorphins make us high and induce a feeling of wellbeing and tranquillity; but as we manufacture endorphins spontaneously within our own bodies, they are legal, safe and non-addictive. (This latter point has been challenged by those who say exercise is addictive and can lead to over-exercising in pursuit of ever-better feelings. Be aware of this, and take note of the safety points listed below).

Taking up exercise can have knock-on benefits in almost every area of your life, apart from relieving stress. Your skin will improve, as will your circulation; your blood pressure lowers. You will find it easier to control your weight, and the body that you have at the moment will become attractively firm and contoured.

To lose weight by restricting your intake of food alone is not only boring and depressing but not, in the long run, that effective. Dieting slows the metabolism, and makes the body hang on harder to the fat reserves it does have. To lose weight by dieting alone you would have to eat a lot less than a person who was watching their food intake but also taking regular exercise; you would eventually, in fact, have to eat at levels that are unhealthy as well as depressing.

People who take up exercise with the aim of losing weight are often pleasantly surprised by how 'normal' their food intake can remain, while still noticing their clothes becoming looser and looser. Exercise boosts your metabolism so that calories are burned more effectively, and your body becomes a more efficient fuel-using 'machine'.

By feeling fit and active, your self-esteem will

improve and you will find your ability to cope with the stresses in your life stronger.

If you choose a team game or a sport such as squash or tennis, your social life will improve too as you meet new people to play with.

The kind of exercise you choose is entirely up to you, but bear in mind that 'regular' exercise is the key. It is reckoned that for improvements in overall fitness to take place, you need to exercise for a minimum of 30 minutes three times a week.

In order to build fitness from scratch, you should probably commit yourself to more than that initially (but take one day off to rest).

Another option is to 'mix and match' your exercise plan. For instance, you might play squash or badminton once a week; swim twice a week; and go for a brisk 40-minute walk on the fourth day.

If at present you are totally unfit and have not exercised for years, start with a gentle activity – walking or swimming – until you build muscle tone and achieve moderate fitness. If you are totally unfit and start off with a high-octane game of squash or an aerobics session you risk injury (which will put you out of action altogether for weeks, and so delay your fitness campaign) and also, if it's too much for you, you risk being put off and deciding not to bother with it again.

Whatever exercise you choose, whether it's sessions in the gym or tennis or swimming or running, enjoy it and do it safely. Here are a few points to remember for very active sports:

● Warm up first by doing simple stretching and bending exercises (such as yoga stretching exercises). Don't go into active exercise without this as cold muscles injure more easily.

● Cool down afterwards – if you're out for a run, slow down on the home stretch, even doing just brisk walking for the last couple of hundred yards.

● Don't get dehydrated: drink plenty of water after exercise.

● Don't exercise within two hours of consuming a heavy meal, and it's best to eat sparingly throughout the day before your exercise session.

● Don't mix alcohol with exercise – it's not just that your performance will be impaired, but exercise allows the alcohol to enter the bloodstream more quickly. It could, in fact, be very dangerous. Have your drink in the bar afterwards.

● If you have a pain, stop at once.

● Don't push yourself too hard. Exercise is meant to be enjoyed, it's not an endurance test. If you are over-tired, or ill, or under the weather – leave it for another day or two and enjoy it all the more when you get back to it.

Walking

I'd like to put in a good word for walking in the exercise stakes. It has much to recommend it. It's free, for a start, and you don't have to buy lycra. A strong and comfy pair of shoes is the only piece of equipment you need – dogs are optional extras, and in the UK a waterproof coat is also a good idea.

There is no age limit, and even the very overweight and unfit can start doing it at once – slowly and gently – and will soon begin to feel the benefits. I know ladies in their 80s who climb Munros (walkable Scottish mountains over 3000 feet) and one 83-year-old who takes her dog for two brisk walks a day and complains of friends younger than herself who can't keep up the pace.

If you're a mum tied to small children, then carry them or push them (that's your weight training bit) until they're old enough to walk and enjoy for themselves.

Walking at a brisk, steady pace increases the heart rate and speeds the metabolism. It is good for your heart, your weight, your breathing, your mood. It lifts the mood, and is not at all dangerous – though take care in narrow country lanes to walk facing oncoming traffic and to the side of the road. On winter walks, wear a light colour and be seen.

If you live in the country, you are rich indeed as your walks bring you into contact with fresh air, the seasons at first hand, with birds and trees and flowers and all the joys of the natural world. If you live in a city, you can really get to know where you live. You can walk to art galleries, rivers, canals, past shops and factories and historic buildings. Look in at your local library to see if they have any leaflets about local canal paths or other designated walkways – it is a dreadful piece of council-speak, but it is nice to know there are proper paths constructed for that brisk hearty walking you want to do. You can join the Ramblers Association, and help keep open those hundreds of footpaths that criss-cross our country – not to mention making new friends. Buy an Ordnance Survey map and find out where these footpaths are.

There are parts of Britain that are certainly over-urban, ugly, industrialised and full of eyesores. But it's a small island, and the miracle is that wherever you are you can almost certainly walk yourself out of it and into something good to look upon.

Relaxation

Contemporary life demands that we drive ourselves hard. In many companies and organisations, longer working hours are the norm: one study suggested that a 1990s employee works on average three hours more per week than a 1960s worker. Getting to and from work, on our congested roads and in crowded public transport, adds hours to the working day and extra notches to the stress levels.

A crucial part of organising your day to maximise stress-relief is to plan the time that you have to yourself.

If you have a 40-minute drive to and from work, and a minimum of a nine-hour day, it may be well after 7pm before you return to your house in the evening. It thus becomes very important that you plan for those hours that belong to you.

You may also have children to care for and other family needs to be met, which – enjoyable though they are – further diminish your available time. It's very tempting, when you're tired and stressed, to pour yourself a large drink and just slump in front of the television, watching whatever is on, too tired to pay much attention.

But over extended periods of time this 'vegging-out' can become more tiring, and a contributory cause of stress, because you are not really relaxing.

Relaxation implies a choice of activity, and that activity needs to be something that actively gives you pleasure and refreshment. We've all had the experience, I'm sure, of coming home from work with a commitment to meet a friend at the cinema or go out for a meal. *'I wish I'd never said I'd go'*, we moan, *'it's the last thing I feel like'*. But we go – and enjoy it very much, because we are actively relaxing.

Give yourself a break

Whether you have a high-stress office job, or work from home, or look after small children all day, it is important to realise that you cannot, with the best will in the world, keep going at a high level of energy all day.

Our initial reaction to stress is that performance is increased. But this increased output is short-term, and gradually performance decreases. At that point, a break is needed.

It's important to listen to our bodies, and be aware of signals that mean our energy levels are dropping. Typically, these are simply feeling tired and sluggish, though all too often we push ourselves on, ignoring what our body is trying to say. Ignoring fatigue quickly allows fatigue to become exhaustion, which takes longer to put right.

We all have our own peaks and troughs, and need to recognise them. For most people, a low point of the day comes in the early afternoon, just after lunch. (This may be because we've eaten too much at lunchtime, in which case try to eat a little less and include more fruit in your diet, or because you have worked through lunch without taking a proper break). Ease off the pressure at this point, and find a mundane task to do that allows your brain to 'switch off' for a while.

It doesn't have to be a long break: 10-20 minutes well used (walking about, getting some fresh air if possible, talking to colleagues, switching to a low-key task such as filing or sorting through your in-tray) will enable you to return to your main task refreshed and more productive.

Smoking

Smoking has become the big no-no in our society. If you smoke, you are already made to feel enough of an outcast and a socially unacceptable pariah (don't you just hate those people who screw up their face and blow the air away in front of you?) without having this book go on at you as well.

You know the facts, and if you don't, a million doctors would just love to tell you. There is overwhelming medical evidence (which even the cigarette manufacturers are now reluctantly being forced to concede) that smoking is a direct cause of many major and life-threatening diseases such as cancer and that it very certainly makes a negative contribution to the development of lots of other unpleasant and debilitating illnesses. In short, if it doesn't actually kill you it can wreck your health to the extent that you might just as well be dead.

If you want to give up (want being the all-important word) you can just go cold turkey: that means, stub out the cigarette in your hand now and never light another one. Lots of people do, and it works for them. Some people cut down, then stop. If you smoke 20 today, allow yourself 15 tomorrow, twelve by Friday. Next week, drop from twelve to five, and so on. Some people need a more distant but specific future goal: I will stop on my birthday.

Nicotine patches are available from chemists, and these work for a lot of people too. There's also hypnosis and acupuncture and chewing gum.

If you have Internet access, log on to Quitnet (www.quitnet.org) which claims to be the world's largest stop-smoking programme. With over 20,000 'members', you will know you are not alone, and the website is full of shared experiences and good ideas from ex-smokers – of which you will soon be one.

Some people find it helpful to put their cigarette money in a jar somewhere – if you have been in the habit of buying 20 cigarettes a day and put that money by, the cash soon piles up. Spend it on a treat, or plan one. People I know who have given up have admitted that they didn't immediately notice a great change in their health (in fact one caught a dreadful cold, and another put on unwanted weight by replacing cigarettes with HobNobs) but they did notice how much cash they suddenly had in their pockets.

Most local health authorities have helplines for would-be quitters, which offer practical advice and support – someone you can ring when you're just dying to have a fag. (Look in *Thomsons* or other local directories). There is almost certainly a notice up in your GPs waiting room about local help available to you, and if there isn't your doctor should be embarrassed about that.

Doctors would advise you to give up now. But, here's a funny thing, lots of doctors and nurses smoke. Why is that? And this, I think, is where a paragraph on smoking becomes relevant in a book about stress. Doctors and nurses – and others working in today's crisis-ridden NHS – are among the most stressed-out, overworked members of society. They know it's bad for them, but by golly it helps them cope – or they think it does.

Smoking has become widely unacceptable in the UK today and there's no doubt that travelling on buses and trains is a lot more pleasant because of it. Pubs that have smoking and non-smoking bars can be assured of a healthy patronage (in both senses of the word) in the non-smoking part. But we're also aware that particularly for young people smoking has an irresistible glamour, in part perhaps of the backlash effect.

The backlash effect is a powerful one. We know how it works with children: absolutely and totally forbid them from doing something because it is unacceptable beyond words, and the net result is that children have an absolute fascination and desire to immediately do that very same thing.

In a stress context, don't beat yourself up if you

smoke and you feel that it really does help you cope. Just be aware that it is in the nature of addictive drugs – and nicotine is just that – to make you dependent on the feeling they give you, and to make you feel that you cannot get by without it.

You can give up. Loads of people have done it and survived and enjoyed better health; you are not alone, and everyone is on your side. If you have friends and peers urging you to smoke, believe me, they are not your friends. Just remember that people generally hate to see someone succeeding at something they know they should be doing themselves.

Alcohol

When the going gets tough, even the tough may hit the bottle. And sometimes, more often than is good for them.

Alcohol is one of the greatest sources of pleasure in this world of ours. What can be nicer than a good bottle of wine with a delicious meal eaten in good company? What better after a hard day at work than to head off to the pub with a bunch of colleagues and enjoy a good hour of complaining and whingeing about the awfulness of work, thereby helping to boost solidarity and put it all in perspective?

Whether you like it or not, the consumption of alcohol does play a major part in the life of this country. It's no accident that *Coronation Street* and *Eastenders* revolve around the Rover's Return and the Queen Vic. Drink is convivial, it brings people together. It's fun. It's celebratory. It's relaxing. It tastes nice. It's legal.

But we also have enough evidence in our daily lives of the damage and the misery it can cause when it all gets out of hand. The 'my booze hell' stories in newspapers, where celebrities chart their decline and fall through drink, may be a cliché but are nonetheless painful; and you don't have to be a footballer or a pop star to be an alcoholic.

The facts are simple. Alcohol is also an addictive drug. Consume it in vast enough quantities, and its effect will be to make you feel you cannot function without it. Its effect is cumulative, in that you need more and more to achieve the same effect: in classical patterns of alcoholism, the drinker switches from 'soft' stuff like beer and wine to hard spirits in order to be able to feel the same kick. And, famously, alcohol is actually a depressant. Initially it may seem to lift the mood (I'll come back to that) but in the long term, the physical effect of heavy duty consumption is a depressant one. There is no such thing as a happy or cheerful alcoholic: what passes for happiness is often the initial heady euphoria with the first few drinks. Make no mistake: after that, it's downhill all the way.

Stress and alcohol is a dangerous combination. Under acute stress, alcohol brings immediate rest, relief and relaxation. It's no accident that people who have suffered a great and sudden shock are usually offered a tot of brandy.

But the person who lives with chronic stress and uses alcohol on a daily basis as a relief for that stress may be heading for trouble. High-stress professions – actors, doctors, lawyers, those who work in the City or competitive big business – or jobs where people may be physically isolated and/or financially anxious (notoriously at this moment farmers) have a high proportion of alcoholics among their ranks. Wealth and a glamorous job are not prerequisites for alcohol abuse. The lonely person on a limited income is equally vulnerable to the warm sense of temporary comfort alcohol can bring.

One woman developed a 'drinking problem' through insomnia brought about by financial worries. Desperately anxious over the situation of her one-woman business, racked by exhaustion after a series of sleepless nights, she found that one or two glasses of wine helped her to sleep better. Within months, this was one or two bottles.

Alcohol was, after all, the first anaesthetic: men facing amputation on the battlefield pleaded for gin to give them oblivion. The story of many alcoholics is of drinking triggered by a bereavement or a personal tragedy, for which alcohol dulled the pain.

I'm painting a gloomy and perhaps extreme picture, but nobody who lives with stress in their lives – and likes a drink – should see themselves as invulnerable. If you do feel that alcohol may be affecting your life, ask yourself these questions:

● Have you ever taken a day off work claiming to be 'ill' when the real cause was a hangover?

● Have you ever sat through a meeting – or just tried to do your normal job – feeling that you would be doing it a lot better if your brain didn't feel fogged by drink?

● Have you ever had a quarrel with a friend which you now feel was fuelled by drink?

● Have you ever woken up in the morning, unable to remember how you got to bed?

● Have you ever gone to bed with someone you never want to see again, and feel now faintly ashamed of having been with, simply because you'd had too much to drink?

● Have you ever gone out for 'just one pint' and mysteriously found yourself hours later, still there, still drinking?

● Have you ever missed an appointment, or let someone down, because you were too busy elsewhere – drinking?

If the answer to all or any of those is yes, perhaps it's time to think about why this is so. There is nothing wrong in using drink to alleviate shock or distress occasionally; but remember that drink can in itself become a problem, replacing and outweighing the original one.

It's useful to have some ways of monitoring your
intake.

● How many alcohol-free days do you have a week?
Do you have any rules for yourself about this? Some
people, for instance, say they won't drink Monday-
Thursday. Some people limit themselves by day (no
more than 1 glass of wine except on Saturdays, no
more than half a pint Mondays through Thursdays,
and so on).

● Can you balance alcohol intake with water and
food? In some countries, alcohol is consumed only
when there's food available to sog it up. If you can't
eat with your drinks, drink lots of water – and
preferably do both.

● Tell yourself you don't drink alone – either at
home or in pubs.

Rules about alcohol intake are hard to keep in
some circles. Some workplaces have a very macho
culture connected with alcohol – the City, for
instance, is known for its work hard, play hard
image, where lunchtime and evening sessions in the
local wine bar are de rigeur. The police force, the
army, builders – traditionally it's been all-male
enclaves where men like to see themselves as tough
and drink is a part of that; but as women seek to be
taken as equals in almost every line of work they,

too, often get drawn into the culture.

Peer pressure should never be underestimated. Heavy drinking because all your workmates do it is not easy to stop: either you stop going out with them, which makes you isolated and different from the people you associate yourself with, or you stand by and drink orange juice, risking the teasing (at best) and ostracism (at worst) that this can bring.

Alcoholics Anonymous, founded in the US in the 1930s, is a unique self-help organisation for alcoholics. It offers unqualified support on a mutual basis for recovering alcoholics, and their twelve-step programme has been widely copied by other organisations helping those with addictions.

AA warn against the HALT syndrome, which may lead recovering alcoholics to pick up a drink again. HALT stands for:

Hungry Angry Lonely Tired

AA members know that if they are feeling any of these emotions, they are particularly vulnerable to picking up a drink. But it's a useful acronym in all sorts of other situations, too.

If you think you occasionally use alcohol in a negative way, ask yourself if you are more likely to start drinking when you are hungry, angry, lonely or tired? As I said above, alcohol is a wonderful mood enhancer. That's why parties are so great and why it's often such a bore to be the one sober person while everyone around you is getting merrier. If you pick up a drink when you're feeling cheerful and upbeat, it can only lift you higher. But if you start to drink because you're feeling angry or weepy or depressed – beware. It can only make it worse.

Getting help for alcohol problems
Alcoholics Anonymous have a 'disease model' of alcoholism which is not to everyone's taste. They say that alcoholics are people with an illness that is incurable; the only coping strategy is to attempt, on a daily basis, never to pick up another drink. No AA member will ever say 'I don't drink' or 'I'll never drink again'. That sort of proud defiant boast is, they know, often the prelude to a binge. Instead they say 'with help, today, just for today, I will not take a drink'.

It may sound austere, but it is a method that has worked for millions of sufferers and their families and made millions of lives worth living.

Going to an AA meeting is not the only way of getting help, and many working in the field of alcohol abuse would say it is not appropriate except for very few long-term chronic abusers. Talk in confidence to your GP about your options, or look in your local *Thomsons* or other directory for confidential helplines.

Another model of alcoholism argues that there are many others who, for a time in their lives, become 'problem drinkers' as a way of coping with a particular set of stressors. While such people should certainly abstain from alcohol while they address those problems and sort their lives out, one day they can start drinking again, in a controlled, wiser way. But this is only after a prolonged period in which they have looked after themselves in a nurturing way, and, with therapeutic help, tried to discover what it was made them drink so much in the first place.

Alcoholics Anonymous: 0345 697555
Drinkline (alcohol counselling and information services): 0345 320202

Debt

At the heart of many stress-related illnesses lies anxiety about money. Either worry about debt makes us ill, or illness leads us into debt.

We live in a consumer-driven society, and it is easy to feel 'deprived' when we look around and see how much other people seem to have. Parents want their children to have what other children have – computers, holidays – even when the money for those things is simply not available.

Single women on low incomes are particularly prone to debt, often because of the compulsive use of credit cards. But in this fashion-conscious world, it is very hard to resist the temptation to buy things we can't really afford, and indeed in many jobs there is a positive pressure to wear different clothes every day.

If debt is causing you anxiety, give yourself a break. Work out now how you can start to deal with the problem. Approach it realistically. There's no point struggling to pay off credit cards in huge lumps if that then leaves you too broke to pay utilities bills or even buy food. *See* Goal setting.

The Citizens' Advice Bureau is a good place to start looking for help and there are now other professional services to give you sound advice and support you as you try to get back on an even keel.

National Debtline: 0645 500511
Alexander Rose Debt Management Ltd: 07000
273583

Sleep

If you're not sleeping properly, the tiniest problems can come to seem huge and insurmountable, and your health will begin to suffer. If you are to cope with the stresses of your life, a priority must be to get a night of restful, dream-filled sleep.

We used to automatically insert 'eight hours' in front of the word sleep but research would seem to show that everyone is different. Mrs Thatcher famously swore by only five hours' sleep a night. Eight hours may be the need for a majority, but we all know people who seem perfectly bouncy on six or seven. Enough sleep is when you wake up feeling rested and can fumble your way to the bathroom and the kettle without an overpowering sense of fatigue and exhaustion.

If you're not sleeping well, try all the old remedies:

● A warm (not hot) bath before you go to bed. Pamper yourself with soap suds and nice smells, and linger in there

● A warm, milky drink. Don't put whisky in it unless you've got a cold. It's a myth that alcohol helps you sleep – it may help you drop off initially, but too much alcohol ensures you will be awake and bouncing off the walls at 3am

● A good book to read is a pleasure; you could of

course try keeping some really dull tome by the bed
to make sure you nod off after a couple of pages

● Put your children safely to bed and forbid them
to disturb you unless it's absolutely essential. The
same with your pets: make them feel loved and
cherished, and shut them in the kitchen with a biscuit.
Many a night's sleep has been ruined for me by an
over-affectionate cat and a dog who occupies the
middle ground of the mattress

● Make sure your bedroom is not too stuffy or too
cold, and that you are warm

● Don't try to sleep. If, after an hour or two of
tossing and turning and clenching your teeth saying 'I
must get to sleep' nothing is happening, stop fighting
it. Get up, make a cup of tea, read your book or the
paper

● If you live alone, watch trashy television in the
early hours – that'll soon have you nodding off.
Persuade your body into leaving you alone by
ignoring the fact that you are not sleeping

It is truly amazing what ills and ailments,
physical and emotional, can be caused or caused by
a lack of sleep – which makes the daylight hours a
nightmare – or by a good restful night.

The wee small hours are notorious: those are
the graveyard hours, when negative thoughts, bad
memories, all our fears and worries burst the

floodgates and take over our minds. That's when you need all your strength to blot them out - imagine the famous *Monty Python* foot stamping them 'thwack'. You have to repeat to yourself, like a mantra, over and over again: I will think about it tomorrow, I will think about it tomorrow, not now, not now, I will think about it tomorrow.

There is nothing you can constructively do when depressed and afraid at 3am to solve your money problems, sort out your relationship, or put matters right at work. Keep a notebook and pen by the bed, however, just in case you do have any brilliant brainstorming ideas and want to make a note of them. Just be firm with yourself: I can do nothing about it now, I am depressed and afraid, I will take care of myself and deal with it tomorrow.

One point: if there is a nagging worry which wakes you at 3am, make sure you do deal with it the next day as best you can. If your bank balance is a mess and there is some practical step you can take to deal with it, or someone who can approach for help and advise, do so. Don't push problems to the back of your life during daylight hours and ignore them – the reason they haunt you in the middle of the night is because it's the only time they can get your attention, and they need it.

Chronic insomnia is very dangerous. Don't

underestimate it. There have been reports of
people who commit suicide after a period of
prolonged insomnia that led to depression. It is
undermining your health, and you need help for it.

Sleeping pills are not a cure, and should not be
used in the long term. Long term, you need to find
a resolution of what it is that forces you awake
when you should be asleep and resting. But in the
short term, see your GP and ask for them; sleep is a
treasure of which you should not be robbed.

List making

Personally, I'm a great fan of list making. I've already decided that when Sue Lawley interviews me for *Desert Island Discs*, my luxury will be a block of A4 paper and a limitless supply of pens, so that I can make lists.

Lists are great stress busters. I have already suggested sitting down with pen and paper and writing a list of all the things you find stressful in your life, and saying whether or not they can be 'cured' or must be 'endured'.

I don't know how people manage without their lists. I know very busy people, frantic with worry, and when you say 'where's your list, then?' they haven't got one.

Writing things down is how to get them into proportion. When you have 20 things to do, write them down and evaluate that list. Prioritise them into urgent, important and – well, the rest of it. Once you know what you must absolutely do now (like pay the gas bill, or it gets cut off), what is important to do (like phone a friend or a relative) and what would be nice to do (like buy some flowers for your sitting room) you can begin to work steadily through that list and have the immense satisfaction of ticking items off as they are done. Don't ever ignore the 'nice to do' things, though – it may not be urgent or important to buy flowers for your house, but they add beauty and give you pleasure, and you should not neglect that.

Writing lists at work can be whittling a stick to beat yourself with. Some people have a list on their desks and are plunged into despair at 4pm when they look at that list and realise that, because of phone calls, interruptions and meetings, they have done nothing on that list. In that case, it's the wrong list. If your working day is crammed with phone calls, interruptions and meetings, it must be because that is an integral part of your job – only you can do that, that is what the job is. (If it really isn't, then for heaven's sake see your boss tomorrow and tell him off for being a lousy manager). 'The list' is just things you will get round to when you have the time, when you are not dealing with urgent and important things.

Look at the list again. Can any of it be delegated? Are there any items on that list that, if not done, will cause the company/organisation/business to eventually grind to a halt? Are there any that, if neglected, will lead to serious problems later on? If so, divert your calls and deal with them now.

I suspect that Type A people have a list full of things they will never get around to because they need the feeling of intense pressure (and importance?) that list creates. Actually most of the things on it are either inessential or could be done by somebody else – Type As just like to be able to hold up their list at 5.40 pm and say 'See! See! I've done none of this!' whereas in fact they have spent the day usefully talking to customers and associates on the phone, giving information and advice, pushing things forward, attending meetings at which they have been able to contribute a great deal, and being interrupted by junior colleagues who needed them to make snap decisions or give instant advice – which they have done. Your Type A, then, may well have had a productive and useful day – but as long as he has this list of not-done things, he will be able to beat himself about the head, feel useless and inadequate, and send his stress levels up another notch or two.

Lists are a useful way of organising the mind. Write things down – and then see whether or not you agree with what you have written. Here is a random list of things you could write a list about:

- Things I like most about my job
- Things I absolutely dislike about my job
- The 20 best things in my life

- Ten things I want to do before I'm 30/40/50/60, etc.

- My best qualities

- My best friends – and what it is I like about them

- My worst qualities – and what I can do (if anything) about them

- What I would do if I had next Monday off

- Books I have never read, but always meant to

There is always a point to these lists. Take the one about your best friends, for instance. If we can distil what it is we like in others, we will often see we have those qualities in ourselves. It's a positive reinforcement. If X is such a great person, they wouldn't have you as a friend unless you were, too, would they?

The reverse may be equally true, and can give us pause for thought. For instance, many of us sometimes maintain a sort-of friendship with people whom we don't actually like at all. This is often a function of low self-esteem. Why do we spend time with X, when objectively we think that person is negative and selfish? Lists are a great way of uncluttering your life.

Happy people have been defined as those with goals, and list-making, after all, is a way of organising your goals: goals for today, goals for the next week or month, goals for the next decade of your life. You may not tick everything off your list; when it comes down to it, you may think they're not so important or interesting after all. The important point is that you do not perceive yourself as helpless and without resources: a person buffeted by life, pulled and pushed by external forces. You're in charge. As the astrologer Jonathan Cainer wrote: Life is choice, not chance.

Laughter

Reader's Digest used to have – probably still does – a section called Laughter, the Best Medicine. It was a page or half a page of silly one-liners, anecdotes, misprints, over-heard-on-a-bus anecdotes, puns, collected and published with the sole aim of providing readers with a chuckle. Laughter is, it seems, if not the best medicine then certainly a very good one – that may be a cliché but as with so mány others, it's based on a known truth.

These days there's even something called laughter therapy and you can attend classes where the whole aim is to teach you to laugh, to loosen up, to really reach within yourself for deep, relaxed, heaving belly laughs. When someone is being too serious we say 'lighten up' and that is precisely what you do when you laugh – not only do you physically relax, but mentally it's as if a load if shifted from your shoulders.

How often has a tense or difficult situation been alleviated by a joke, a giggle, a shared sense of fun?

Leslie Kenton, writer of many wise books on self-help and health, advocates keeping a folder of things that make you laugh – cartoons from the paper, jokes, anecdotes. Add to that a stock of videos of films or television classics guaranteed to make you laugh – a resource you can turn to when only Fawlty Towers or It'll be All Right on the Night can put the day into perspective.

The British are renowned for their self-deprecating sense of humour and if that's so then we should prize it and cultivate it. In trying to see the humorous side of things we're not denying their essential gravity. Sometimes the very best comedy – think of the *Blackadder* series set during World War I – can make serious and hard-hitting points about tragically real issues. Think of the black humour that existed during wartime, among pilots about to fly off on dangerous missions. In such circumstances, humour is a safety valve, a defence mechanism, a way of getting through awful times. It's also something more than that: a way of showing personal courage, of encouraging others, of keeping balance in a perilously tilting world.

Real humour is not cruel. Jokes that depend for their punchline on cruelty towards others, or racism, or sexism or homophobia are not real humour at all. Forget about cheap comedians who use their art as a way of putting others down. True humour is compassionate, and celebrates life in all its weird diversity and difference. True humour punctures pomposity, and only puts down (wittily, with fun not viciousness) those who have so puffed themselves up they deserve it.

Oscar Wilde, a man whose clever plays have generated laughter for a century, and who suffered imprisonment, exile and humiliation in his private life, wrote: 'We are all in the gutter, but some of us are looking at the stars'.

Seriousness is a lonely business; humour binds us to other people, and in laughter we can look beyond our own immediate predicaments and perhaps even up at the stars too.

COMPLEMENTARY THERAPIES

I am deliberately using the term 'complementary' rather than 'alternative' therapies. Complementary means 'completing; together making up a whole' and in most cases these therapies should not be regarded as replacements for conventional medicine, but supplements and enhancements to it. The word complementary has also come to mean free, which these therapies aren't, although some General Practices now directly refer patients to practitioners such as acupuncturists or aromatherapists.

If you have stress in your life because of a medical condition, your first port of call should be to your doctor. He or she may well encourage you to use a complementary therapy, either instead of or as well as conventional medication.

Always tell your complementary therapist if you are on any medication – they usually ask anyway – or if you are, or think you may be, pregnant.

On no account should you stop taking medicine prescribed by your doctor, or even reduce the dosage, without consulting him first.

One story I particularly like is of a courageous elderly lady who had suffered the double tragedy of a bereavement in her life followed by a stroke which partially paralysed her. For several years her doctor treated her with anti-depressants and sleeping tablets. Then she became interested in Buddhism and also in the Alexander Technique. She took up meditation to find inner tranquillity and Alexander Technique helped her regain strength and balance. During a routine check-up with her doctor he marvelled at how well she seemed and she told him about her new interests. 'Well', he said smiling, 'I don't suppose you'll need me much any more'.

Traditional Chinese medicine (TCM)
The practice of TCM has not yet grown in the West to the same extent that many of its complementary healing methods such as acupuncture and shiatsu have. But a note about some of its basic philosophies may be useful.

Some 2500 years ago, Taoist priests in Northern China practised Chi Gong (which is now beginning to be introduced in Britain). This is a purposeful, focused form of movement (not unlike T'ai Chi) which aims at nurturing the life force, called variously Chi or Qi (it has several different pronunciations and spellings). This life force animates the whole universe, flowing through every living thing and every natural phenomenon.

This 'life force' has no real equivalent in Western medicine, which grew out of non-spiritual roots. At some point in the history of the West, body and spirit parted company: doctors treat the body, while religions treat the spirit - often trying to pretend the body does not exist. This separation never took place in the Eastern tradition.

Unlike Western medicine, which only cures the body once illness has become manifest, TCM aims at preserving health in the body so that illness will not occur.

The life force is made up of opposites: yin (traditionally associated with the feminine and connected with earth, darkness and passivity) and yang (the masculine, positive and dynamic, associated with heaven and light). As with night and day, heat and cold, sweet and acid, all opposites are necessary and complementary, and in accepting one we must accept its opposite. We cannot love the day without accepting the existence too of night.

Such a philosophy also accepts that everything is constantly in a state of motion. At the darkest moment of night, we are already moving towards the dawn.

Chi flows through the human body as blood flows through our veins. Just as unimpeded blood flow is necessary for optimum health (and disorders of the blood cause disease or illness), exactly the same with Chi. Twelve channels called meridians, carry Chi round the body – six carry yin, and six carry yang. Good health depends upon a balance between yin and yang.

TCM has something of a mixed reputation in Britain, not least because some pills and powders used in the practice of it have been linked with the destruction of rare animals such as the tiger. For our purposes here, it is only necessary to have an understanding of the basic and ancient principles of it. The herbal and homeopathic systems of medicine described below, as well as the healing methods, have at their heart a reverence for human and animal life, and an antipathy towards mindless destruction. As in every philosophy, bad practice may and can creep in.

Aromatherapy

The human sense of smell is actually very keen, although for most of us nowadays we only notice smells when they are unpleasant. In pre-historic days our sense of smell was as crucial to survival as it is for animals in the wild today, used for smelling intruders and enemies by their odour.

We forget how smell can affect mood. It's now something of a joke that if you're trying to sell your house you should contrive to have it smelling of fresh-ground coffee, newly baked bread and fresh flowers when showing it to potential buyers but there is an entirely serious point behind it. Those smells are variously associated with a comfortable and welcoming home and that's exactly the kind of mood you want to create.

Smells have a memory, too. For some people, the smell of new-mown grass will take them back to schooldays when playing fields were regularly cut, just as much as the smell of ink or plimsolls or boiled cabbage. To me the scent of lavender instantly reminds me of my grandmother, while herbs on a sunny window-sill transport me in spirit at least to the hillsides of Greece.

The art of aromatherapy is to use essential oils to promote a sense of wellbeing and serenity. The aroma is inhaled and affects the nervous system and the brain through stimulating the olfactory nerves. If used directly on the skin (in minute and controlled quantities, preferably by a proper practitioner during a massage) the oils enter the bloodstream and the effect is heightened.

The use of oils for therapeutic purposes was known by the ancient Egyptians. In 1000 AD a Persian doctor is recorded as distilling fragrant oils from plants and mixing them with oil (probably castor or olive) to make soothing lotions.

Through trade with the Greeks and Romans the art came to Britain and was written about in the 13th century. But as the world became more interested in synthetic copies of real substances in later centuries, interest in aromatherapy waned. Early in the twentieth century a French chemist used lavender oil for a burn on his hand, and from that incident we can date the revival of modern aromatherapy.

The oils – and over 70 are known about, though comparatively fewer are in regular use – can be used in one of three ways.

Massage
If you contact a professional aromatherapist, this is the most likely form of treatment you will have. It's a good idea to be introduced to aromatherapy this

way because the therapist will not only be an expert in which oils to use, but will also know how to give a really good massage!

You can of course ask a friend or partner to give you a massage at home, or massage parts of your own body, but a word of warning: essential oils should never be used directly on the skin and it is important to prepare them properly. They need to be mixed with a 'carrier oil' that will dilute their powerful effect. All herbalists and chemists that sell aromatherapy oils will sell carrier oils; usually these are grapeseed or almond oil and the dilution instructions on the oil itself should be followed. Don't think that by adding extra oil you will have a more beneficial effect as this is not the case: all you may end up doing is causing a skin irritation or rash.

Massaging your neck and shoulders is wonderful for unravelling the knots of tension that build up there during the day. A gentle massage on the temples can ease the pain of a headache and if you've been on your feet all day you can give yourself a leg or foot massage.

In the bath
A simple tonic is to add 6-8 drops of an essential oil to a warm (not hot) bath. Then place a warm facecloth over your face, lie back and relax.

Inhaling oils

Many shops - gift shops, health shops, herbalists, chemists - sell diffusers, burners and vaporisers. These are all devices into which you can add oils and then warm the device, usually by a small candle or by placing it over a light bulb on a lamp, so that the warmed oil evaporates and the aroma permeates the room. The smell is wonderful and soothing by itself, but if you regularly meditate or do any kind of relaxation technique such as visualisation, then burning an essential oil while you do this can enhance the sense of calm.

The oils listed are a very, very small selection. An aromatherapist, or a detailed book on aromatherapy, will point you in the direction of oils that can help alleviate your specific problem, be it PMT or dry skin or headaches.

Warning: Aromatherapy is a lot of fun and the oils smell glorious, but treat them all with caution. They are powerful substances and not just ordinary bath oil. Some of them should not be used in pregnancy or by children under the age of 5; some of them may cause problems to asthmatics or epileptics. Always read the label carefully on any oil you buy and use it as instructed.

Some commonly used essential oils are as follows.

Name	Recommended for
Bergamot	Antiseptic and uplifting; recommended in a burner for getting rid of nasty niffs in the house. Be careful in the sun, though, as bergamot can increase the risk of sunburn
Clary sage	Recommended for use in PMT because of its soothing and comforting qualities; aromatherapists also massage the tummy area with it for period pain
Cypress	Has cleansing and antiseptic properties
Eucalyptus	With lemon, excellent for clearing the head
Fennel	Good for the digestion and has been recommended for breast firming and milk production, but you should not use it if you are pregnant
Frankincense	One of the gifts brought by the Three Wise Men, the ancient Egyptians thought it had rejuvenating properties; it certainly has a comforting and calming effect with a rich and warm aroma
Geranium	Promotes a sense of balance; used in treating eczema and other skin conditions

Name	Recommended for
Ginger	Alleviates nausea and sickness, so try this in a bath for flu or hangovers
Hyssop	A very powerful oil which should be used carefully but is great for colds and flu; thought to cleanse rooms from infection, which is why the ancient Greeks used hyssop brooms to sweep their temples
Juniper	Thought to strengthen the immune system
Peppermint	Excellent for making you feel fresh, alert and clear-headed; add a few drops to the morning bath for a zestful start to the day
Roman chamomile	Encourages a relaxed mood and has a generally soothing effect; good for insomnia. Unlike many other essential oils, it may be used on irritated skin but should not be used in early pregnancy.
Tea tree	Because of its antiseptic and antifungal properties, this is now used in a wide range of cosmetic products
Thyme	Good for relieving head colds

Further reading
Julia Lawless, *The Complete Illustrated Guide to Aromatherapy*. Element.
Robert Tisserand, *The Art of Aromatherapy*. Daniel.

Massage

Several of the complementary therapies described below involve forms of massage. Massage has been known as an art for thousands of years, and indeed in ancient times and other cultures you did not have to be in pain or sore after physical exercise to seek a massage: it was just a normal part of the routine of looking after oneself.

Being massaged is one of the most comforting of stress-relievers – right from the time our mothers comforted us as babies by rubbing our backs for 'wind' or stroked us to soothe us to sleep, we have responded to gentle, rhythmic touch. It's a natural response to touch a part of the body that hurts, and rub it to bring relief from pain. Touch calms, and reduces our sense of inner loneliness and isolation.

Professional massage obviously has much to recommend it, but there are things we can do at home that also soothe.

There are three basic movements involved in massage: stroking, with a movement as if you were peeling the pain and stress away from an area of the body; kneading, which is exactly as if you were kneading a part of the body with your whole hand like a lump of dough; and friction, using the thumbs, the tips of the fingers or the heel of the

hand in circular motions or in straight lines.
Imagine with this movement that tension is stuck
inside the muscle and you are trying to tease it out
with your fingers, as if a splinter is stuck in there
and you can bring it to the surface.

On your own, there are obviously not many
parts of yourself that you can reach to massage:
your head, your temples, your face, your legs and
feet, but even so if you feel particularly stressed, try
to make some time to lie down on the floor,
propped up with cushions if you need to. Use
attractively scented oils to make the experience
more sensual and pleasurable. Turn the lights
down or out, and light candles. Play soothing
music, or enjoy silence. Then, using a mixture of
the three movements described above, work on
parts of your body, kneading, stroking and
pressing-and-circling.

Don't worry if you feel this is not 'real massage'.
First, you will be soothing and calming yourself,
which is important; and you are focusing wholly on
yourself, which you need to do from time to time.
Physically, massage increases blood circulation and
causes dilation of the blood vessels; it also
stimulates lymphatic drainage. (This means the
process by which waste substances and toxins are
flushed away from the body's tissues by the

lymphatic system).

If you have a partner or a friend willing to help you, so much the better: you can massage each other.

All parts of the body benefit, but stress has a way of knotting up the neck and the back, so working on these areas is a wonderful release.

Neck massage - Sit on a chair with your back straight, so that your partner can stand behind you. The massage should begin with stroking movements but start at the bottom of the shoulder blades and work up each side of the spine to the nape of the neck. Pull your hands apart across the top of the shoulders and bring them down again to the position you started from. Then, using the fingers and thumbs, exert pressure on the shoulders – think of the way cats use their claws in a pressing motion. Finally, use strong kneading motions on the shoulders. The person having the massage will certainly be able to tell the masseur what feels good, and restful!

Back massage - Follow the cocktail of movements outlined above when working on the back. The person having the massage should lie flat on the floor on a towel, or a bed (but it should be firm). The arms should either be folded under the chin and face to support them, or stretched out above the head. The masseur can really apply his or her own body weight in massaging the back. Start at the base of the spine, and work up to the shoulders. It is particularly beneficial to press the 'channels' on either side of the spine on the upper back.

When giving a massage, make your movements as calm, unhurried and focused as possible. Try not to lift your hands from the other person's body. The aim is obviously not to be rough or to hurt, but neither should you be too gentle. Imagine that you can literally draw tension out of the other person, like pulling a hand out of a glove, or getting a foot out of a tight boot, and so the pressure needs to be firm enough to do so.

Reflexology

Tomb paintings dated 2330 BC showing what looks like the practice of reflexology have been found in Egypt, and certainly the art of massaging feet therapeutically has been known for many thousands of years.

The modern practice of reflexology works from the principle that the whole body is divided into ten zones. The life force – variously called simply energy, or Chi or kundalini in other cultures – flows through these zones of the body; stress or illness cause blockages and so the flow of the life force is impeded just as if a river is dammed. By massaging the feet in a particular way, the reflexologist breaks down this blockage and releases the tension.

Every part of the foot is believed to be linked with a particular part of the body. In a reflexology massage the therapist will work on all parts of the foot, but some may be more sensitive than others if there is a problem in that area. Pre-menstrual women, for example, may find that when that part of the foot relating to the abdomen is touched, they experience slight discomfort.

Many people have no interest in reflexology for therapeutic purposes, they just go to enjoy a thoroughly relaxing massage that soothes and calms. Most people find they sleep like a log after the initial session, although the effect is cumulative. For mild conditions (or just as a beneficial massage) most therapists recommend a course of 6 weekly sessions, followed by a once-a-month top up.

There are reports that conditions such as PMS, diabetes, arthritis, stress, headaches and digestive problems have benefited from reflexology sessions. For those with long-term illnesses, such as multiple sclerosis, regular sessions can help promote sleep and release the tensions that build up in the chronically ill. Because it induces deep relaxation, it can help with pain. (My first experience of reflexology was at a time when I was in great pain from an abscessed tooth; the pain almost vanished).

Reflexology is particularly helpful with elderly people or those for whom the idea of a full-body massage (which involves removing clothes) is distasteful. Reflexology is just as therapeutic as a full body massage (some would claim more so) but all you need take off are shoes and socks or stockings. The therapist will usually cover the calves and ankles with a towel and, as a special bonus, often uses aromatic creams or lotions on the feet as well!

Further reading

Inge Dougans and Peter Bridgewater, *The Complete Illustrated Guide to Reflexology.* Element.

Ann Gillanders, *Gateways to Health and Harmony with Reflexology.* British School of Reflexology.

Nicola M. Hall, *Principles of Reflexology.* Thorsons.

Herbal medicine

In the story of our life on this planet, humans have been using today's chemical, synthetic drugs for a period equivalent to the blink of an eye. In the hundreds of centuries before today's pills and tablets, people relied on herbs and plants that grew wild and free for their medicine. There are written Chinese records of herbal remedies which are 5000 years old, and the use of herbs in medicine was common throughout India and the Middle East for centuries before returning Crusaders brought some of this knowledge back to Britain in the Middle Ages.

Nicholas Culpeper (1616-1654) is probably the most famous name in British herbalism; his book *The Complete Herbal* was published in 1653 and many of the remedies he specifies are still in use today.

There are many people who dismiss herbal medicine as 'old wives' tales' but forget that many drugs we use today are based on compounds which mimic those occurring naturally in the plant world. Salicylic acid, found in the white willow, is the basis for aspirin, for instance; the heart drug digitalis is made from foxglove leaves. More recently, the 'wonder drug' Taxol used in the treatment of cancer was originally found in the bark of a rare yew tree in California, while the anti-depressant Prozac contains a substance that occurs naturally in St John's Wort.

Herbal medicine has endured for centuries, and the fact that it has not been entirely replaced by conventional medicine speaks for its efficacy.

Herbal treatments are particularly useful in any condition arising from nervous stress or tension: digestive upsets, for instance, colitis, ulcers or even irritable bowel syndrome. One of the main digestive juices in our system is hydrochloric acid. In the depressed person, secretion of this acid is reduced, so we digest food less efficiently. When we are under stress the release of adrenaline leads to an over-production of hydrochloric acid, and this can have an irritant effect on pre-existing gut conditions such as ulcers.

Remedies are now sold over the counter in health food shops and herbalists, as well as some chemists. Certain 'mild' remedies for mild conditions are well known, see table opposite:

Over-the-counter remedies are available as pills, creams or lotions, and many of them are 'combination products' containing a variety of ingredients, so you ask the shop assistant for a remedy for the condition you have, rather than an actual herb. Quiet Life tablets, for instance, which

Remedy	Used for
Pulsatilla	Styes, earache, PMS
Nux. vom	Hangovers, insomnia
Apis. mel	Cystitis, bladder problems
Acid. phos	Indigestion, wind
Cocculus	Nausea, vomiting
Arnica	Fatigue, toothache
Ignatia	Headache
Nat. mur.	Colds and flu
Euphrasia	Hayfever
Catarrh	Kali. bich.

are said to help relieve anxiety and calm the nerves, contain wild lettuce, motherwort, hops and valerian. Boots Herbal Water Relief tablets, which claim to help women who suffer from water retention before their period, contain burdock root and uva ursi among other herbs.

These remedies can help, but if your condition is more serious and you want individual advice, contact a good herbalist and arrange to have an individual session with a trained and qualified herbalist.

Shiatsu

The word shiatsu is literally translated from the Japanese as 'finger pressure'. The belief on which it is based is that Chi – the life force – flows through all parts of the body along channels that are known as meridians. When this life force becomes blocked or slowed, illness occurs. In order for the individual to feel well, the life force must flow brisk and clear, and shiatsu is a form of massage that encourages this process.

Using his or her fingers (though thumbs, knees and feet can also be used in more vigorous forms!) the shiatsu therapist kneads the body like bread, gently and rhythmically encouraging the flow of Chi and the restoration of balance.

How is this different from an ordinary massage? The answer, as with all these ancient therapies, is that it is a 'holistic' therapy. That is, the shiatsu practitioner will be interested in the whole client – what you eat, what your habits are, and the state of your physical and mental health. To fully benefit from shiatsu (and indeed from any holistic therapy) you should not expect just to turn up, pay the fee and have a good massage. The practitioner is truly concerned to encourage you to transform your life by changing habits that harm your health and adopt others that benefit you.

Another interesting aspect is the sense of personal responsibility that holistic therapies such as shiatsu expect. In more conventional therapies, the client is passive and has a therapy 'done to' them. Holistic therapies engage the client as a full partner in the process, taking responsibility for their own health and the decisions made in daily life which affect it.

Further Reading
Elaine Liechti, *The Complete Illustrated Guide to Shiatsu.* Element.

Acupuncture

This is the traditional Chinese therapy that uses
very fine, long needles inserted at specific points on
the body to achieve a specific effect. As with
shiatsu, the theory is that these needles unblock the
meridians (or channels) of the body, thus enabling
Chi (the life force) to move freely and actively and
restore the body to total health. In addition,
placing pressure on certain parts of the body (this
is called acupressure if done with the fingers and
acupuncture if done with needles) relieves pain.

Although acupuncture has been used in China
for centuries it is still used there today. Some years
ago amazing film was shown on television of a man
having surgery during which acupuncture and not
anaesthetic drugs were used for controlling pain.
The patient was fully awake, sipping tea and
chatting with the surgeons, while undergoing
abdominal surgery. (This is definitely not one to
try at home).

In rather less drastic circumstances, many
people have found pain relief with acupuncture for
conditions ranging from stiff necks to bad backs,
period pain, migraine and arthritic pain. Many
people have also been helped to give up smoking
by acupuncture needles placed, oddly enough,
behind the ear. A number of GP surgeries now

make acupuncture available to patients who would prefer to try this method of relief before resorting to drugs. The great advantage of acupuncture over drugs is, of course, that there are no unpleasant side effects.

Bach Flower Remedies

A London homeopath, Dr Edward Bach, developed these simple remedies in the 1930s and today they have an enormously loyal and dedicated following.

Bach began with the theory (easy enough to comprehend) that flowers not only calm our minds but have an effect on physical wellbeing too. It's no accident that we traditionally carry flowers to a sick person, or comfort the bereaved with them as a token of love for the dead. Bach's remedies are made in Oxfordshire from plant or flower extracts: there are 38 of them, each one created for a specific ailment or condition. The collective aim of them all is to restore balance or harmony and overcome the negative emotions that Bach believed led to illness.

The remedies are widely available in health food shops, herbalists and some chemists such as Boots. There is always literature and instructions with the display of remedies to direct you to the appropriate one, and often you may need to mix and match. For the first time, it's probably best to purchase them from a shop where the assistant knows about Flower Remedies and can give you good advice.

The drops themselves are diluted in water and then placed directly on the tongue.

'Remedies' is a lovely cosy old-fashioned word

implying instant comfort and that's exactly what the Flower Remedies are - a sort of herbal version of chicken soup or a mug of hot chocolate.

In particular, Bach's Rescue Remedy should be in everyone's medicine chest. Its ingredients include star of Bethlehem, rock rose and clematis and it is intended as an immediate first-aid in moments of stress or shock – for instance with the sudden pain of a burn, cut or other household accident. Many people also find them helpful when confronted with a psychological shock or stressful event.

Pet therapy

The role of pets in human life for inducing calm and promoting wellbeing has been highlighted in recent years. Dogs have for centuries had a working role, of course, as sheepdogs, guard dogs and latterly as guide dogs for the blind. Today dogs are also trained to help deaf people and housebound people confined to wheelchairs - dogs can open and close doors, carry quite heavy objects, and be relied upon to attract attention in a variety of ways when they sense that their owner needs help from other sources.

Studies report that people who own cats or dogs (and other animals, of course, but mainly either of these two) tend to be less stressed than those who don't. The reasons are clear to those who love animals anyway: who could be stressed with a cat around, when cats themselves are the most serene, contemplative of animals? Animals are companions who don't judge: neither your cat nor your dog cares how much you earn, what your job title is, whether the world considers you a success or a failure.

In looking after our animals, we learn to be simpler, and less selfish.

Dogs can be as demanding of time and attention as a small child, and are not recommended for people who work full-time away from the home. It is frankly cruel to leave a dog alone at home for periods longer than about 4-5 hours. But dogs love their owners unconditionally, and the affection and companionship they offer – for very little return – is attested to by millions of devoted dog owners.

A happy innovation in recent years has been the number of old people's homes and nursing homes where pets are allowed and even encouraged. Unless people are clinically ill (when an antiseptic distance from animals might become an issue) it has been proved time and time again that the bedridden, chairbound or immobile love to pet and stroke animals and to watch their antics.

Transcendental meditation (TM)

TM came to prominence (or notoriety) in the
1960s, when the Beatles learned the technique
direct from the guru Maharishi Mahesh Yogi. That
ballyhoo has long since died down, but thousands
of people still practice TM daily and vouch for its
usefulness in relieving stress. It has been described
as a 'mental bath', clearing the head and leaving the
meditator refreshed and motivated.

TM is not a religion. Meditators are instructed
in the technique by an accredited teacher of TM,
and are given a mantra – usually a word in
Sanskrit. This mantra is wholly theirs, and in two
20-minute sessions a day (the recommended
amount) the mantra is repeated internally over and
over again until calm is induced.

In the UK, over 700 doctors practice Transcendental meditation every day and recommend it
to their patients. One health insurance company in
Canada offered a 50 per cent discount for anyone
practising TM because research has shown that
mediators make 50 per cent fewer claims than non-
meditators. It is expensive, however, and many
question that something so apparently simple and
beneficial should be made somewhat exclusive by
its cost.

Studies have revealed that TM is helpful in all

stress-related disorders such as angina, high blood pressure, anxiety, depression and insomnia.

For information on learning TM, call: 0990 143 733

Homeopathy

Conventional medicine is called 'allopathy' from the Greek words meaning 'the opposite cures', meaning that most of Western medicine as we know it consists of finding an antidote for whatever condition you have. The word 'homeopathy' comes from Greek words meaning 'suffer the same' and the underlying principle of homeopathy may be expressed as: Let like be cured by like.

The ancient Greek physician Hippocrates mentioned homeopathy, but it wasn't until the eighteenth century that a German, Samuel Hahnemann, rediscovered and developed it into its present form.

The theory of homeopathy is that it works by giving the patient infinitesimally small doses of some curious substances that can, in large doses, produce the same symptoms as the condition from which the patient is suffering. In other words, a substance that is naturally poisonous in a large dose, can in a very small dose be curative. Hahnemann tested his theories on himself – originally by taking quinine in a variety of doses for malaria – and this self-testing is still common practice among homeopaths. Homeopathic remedies are not tested on animals, although some vets now practice homeopathic medicine and the remedies are available in doses suitable for animals.

Homeopaths believe that when the body is out of balance it becomes ill. Symptoms such as rash or fever indicate that the immune system is marshalling all its resources to fight the disease. By administering tiny doses of a substance that will produce similar symptoms to the illness itself, this adds to the resources the body has to fight the illness. Some remedies sound very strange indeed: snake, arsenic, gold, silica.

Making an appointment with a homeopath will lead to a very different experience from seeing a conventional doctor. As we all know, conventional doctors make appointments at five or ten minute intervals, and their main concern as you walk through the door is to find out what part of the body hurts so that they can write an appropriate prescription for you to take away with you – or make an appointment for you to see a specialist in that body part.

Your initial appointment with a homeopath will usually be for one hour, and subsequent appointments are seldom less than 30 minutes. This is because homeopathy is a holistic form of medicine: the practitioner is interested in the whole person, not just the body part that appears to be ailing. Therefore the homeopath will begin by taking a detailed history of your life – what you eat, how you sleep, your lifestyle, past illnesses, your mental as well as your physical state of health.

The remedies are usually given as tiny tablets though liquid or powder forms of the substance may be used in the homeopathic practice – remedies you buy from a herbalist, homeopathic pharmacy or health shop will usually be in tablet form. The dose is so small that it's best to avoid touching the tablets with your hands at all in case of contamination. Most homeopaths recommend you drop a pill into the cap of the bottle and then pop it straight on your tongue without finger contact.

The remedies have no side effects and are non-addictive, and may even be taken at the same time as conventional medicines. (A homeopath would certainly not advise you to give up conventional medicines you are taking). As they are so powerful, it is often the case that only one dose is needed. Unlike conventional medicine, where doctors advise you to finish the course (or bottle of tablets) and treatments can be very long drawn-out, homeopaths work with single doses or very short courses of a tablet or ointment. The remedies are available in a variety of strengths (that is, according to the dilution) and these are called 'potencies'. If you buy them over the counter, be sure to ask for advice on which potency is best for you.

You should not put anything at all in your mouth for 20 minutes before and after taking a homeopathic remedy. This includes drinking, eating, smoking, chewing gum or cleaning your teeth.

Who consults homeopaths? Anybody and everybody with a condition or ailment that does not require surgery. So they can't help with broken limbs or malignancies that must be excised by surgery – though remedies can help with knitting bone together, wound healing and with pain relief. Patients with skin conditions, respiratory ailments, PMS, stress-related conditions, digestive problems and bladder complaints have all benefited from the use of homeopathic remedies. Europeans (especially the French) have been using them on an everyday basis long before they became popular in the UK – although it's said that the Royal Family have been consulting homeopathic doctors for years.

The table below lists some commonly available remedies and the conditions they're used for – but there are many, many more and there are usually several possible remedies for one condition. The best thing is to find a homeopathic pharmacy or good herbalist near you and go and talk to them.

Remedy	used for
Camomile Tea	soothing, relaxing, inducing sleep
Peppermint Tea	digestive discomforts such as wind, or after over-eating
Slippery elm tablets	gastric upsets
Arnica (usually as a cream)	bruises
Calendula (usually as a cream)	sore and rough skin
Echinacea	strengthens the immune system
Valerian	promotes sleep
Vervain	headaches

Further reading

Andrew Lockie and Nicola Geddes, *The Complete Guide to Homepathy*. Dorling Kindersley.

Cassandra Marks, *In a Nutshell: Homeopathy*. Element.

Wayne B Jonas and Jennifer Jacobs, *Healing with Homeopathy*. Time Warner.

Yoga

The word yoga comes from the Sanskrit for 'union'. Known and practised for over 3000 years, yoga is a discipline that unites mind and body, seeing one as a mirror of the other. It is a philosophy of balance and wholeness. A 'true' study of yoga is long term and serious, involving mental as well as physical disciplines.

In recent years in the West yoga has become a mainstay of evening classes and keep-fit centres, but even in this somewhat diluted form it has brought relaxation and a sense of wellbeing to thousands.

There are various forms of yoga, but the most commonly practised is hatha yoga which uses asanas (physical postures) and pranayamas (breathing techniques) to induce calm and encourage a focus on the inner moment (hatha means sun and moon). For those under stress, the breathing techniques alone (yoga breaths are through the nostrils, deep and slow) can bring benefits. Other forms taught in the UK include Iyenagar yoga (recommended for bad backs as foam pads are used to prevent injury), Viniyoga (which places greater emphasis on breathing) and Ashtanga Vinyasa (often recommended for mountaineers and those who partake in high-energy, high-risk sports).

Although many study yoga for its spiritual dimension, some do so simply for the physical agility and suppleness it develops. After its heyday of popularity in the 60s when yoga was very much a hippy thing, yoga is now seeing something of a revival with Sting, footballer David Ginola, actor Woody Harrelson and singer Robbie Williams among its adherents.

Yoga is the ideal form of relaxation for stressed people. It has to be done in a still, quiet place; you have to be comfortable; and it is quality Me Time.

Although there are many excellent books available, with full colour photographs demonstrating various yoga poses, the best way to start is still to find a teacher or a class locally and go along. That way you will see yoga in action, practised by the teacher, and have some individual help in moving the body into positions that may be new and strange to you, without force or injury.

Here, though, are a few basic exercises to get you started. As with all forms of exercise, remember to follow these rules:

- Wear loose, comfortable clothes
- You'll need sufficient floor space to spread

yourself out. Use a mat or rug if you are on a hardwood floor, to avoid injury

● Do not get dehydrated; take sips of room-temperature water while exercising, and drink lots of water afterwards

● If you feel pain, stop. You should not force these positions so that you are uncomfortable or in pain. Gradually, as you become supple, your body will become more and more used to them

● Don't forget to breathe all the time!

Stretching
1. Sit cross-legged on the floor. (These exercises should be done in the Half-Lotus position, but this is not easy for beginners, and takes years of practice). If this is not comfortable for you, place a cushion or a foam pad under your bottom.
2. With your palms facing upwards, lift your arms until you can press your hands together above your head, as if you were praying. Breathe in all the time you are raising your hands. Press your palms together and be aware of stretching, as if you were trying to lift your whole body.
3. Slowly lower your arms, breathing out.
4. Repeat three times.
5. Now raise your arms until they are horizontal, with the palms facing downwards.
6. Breathe in, look at your left hand, and turn your

body to the left, keeping your legs still. Breathe out as you slowly return to the centre.

7. Repeat the same movement, turning to the right.

The Cat

1. Sit on your heels and place your arms on the ground in front of you, elbows touching your knees, palms face down on the floor.

2. Gently raise yourself up on to all fours, raising hips and shoulders and straightening (but not locking) your arms.

3. Drop your head between your arms and arch your back as a cat does when stretching. Breathe out as you arch your back.

4. Breathe in and drop your chest slightly as you bend your elbows and lift your head. Hold your breath for as long as is comfortable then breathe out and arch your back again, as you did in step 3.

5. Repeat this twice.

The Triangle

1. Stand with your feet hip width apart and your toes pointing forward.

2. Keep your left foot pointing forwards, but turn your right foot 90 degrees to the right, so that it is pointing as far as possible to your right. Keep your hips still and pointing forwards.

3. Breathe in, and raise your arms sideways to shoulder height.

4. Breathing out, slowly bend so that your right arm is touching your right ankle, while your left arms reaches above your head.

5. Your left arm should form almost a straight line with your left. Don't worry if you can't reach your ankle for a while, just run your right arm as far down your right leg as it will comfortably go.

6. Breathe in, and slowly come upright. Then turn your feet round the opposite way, and repeat by reaching for the left ankle with the left hand.

The Sun Salutation
These poses should follow each other in a simple, fluid motion.

1. Stand straight but relaxed, with your feet touching and your hands pressed together on your chest in the prayer pose (nemaste). Breathe in.

2. Breathing out, bend slightly forward, linking your right thumb over your left. Stretch your arms forward then raise them over your head, breathe in again and arch backwards as far as is comfortable, pushing your pelvis slightly forward.

3. Come back to the vertical, breathe in, and bend forward from the waist until your hands touch your feet. This may not be possible until you've had some practice and are more supple, so don't force it.

4. Breathe in, stretch your left leg out behind you (toes tucked under), and crouch on to your right knee. Look up.

5.Breathe in and stretch both legs out behind you, keeping your body in a straight line and supporting your weight on your hands and your toes. Keep breathing in and out.

6. Breathe out and drop your knees and chest to the floor. Your hips should be slightly raised and your toes still tucked under.

7. Now press down with your hands, raise your head and your chest, keep your hips on the ground, elbows bent and feet stretched back (your toes are not tucked under at this stage). Your head will be thrown back as if you were feeling the sun on it.

8. Come up into an arch: that is, your hands and feet on the ground, making an archway with your bottom.

9. Repeat stage 4, but this time it's your right leg that is stretched out behind you, and your left foot that is resting between your hands under your chest.

10. Straighten your right leg and place your feet together, breathing out. Lift your buttocks, so that your head and arms fall forward. If possible, touch the ground with your fingers.

11. Slowly lift yourself and arch backwards, raising your arms over your head, lifting your face, as if to adopt an attitude of prayer to the sun.

12. Lower your arms and brings your hands back into the prayer position, palms pressed together. Your head should be looking straight forward.

It is recommended that once you are familiar with this complete routine, you should start your day by practising it several times.

There are addresses of yoga associations and further contacts at the end of this book.

Further Reading
Swami Shivapremananda, *Yoga for Stress Relief.*
Gaia.

T'ai Chi

T'ai Chi has been described as meditation in action. It is a slow, dance-like form of creative movement in which the participant makes a series of movements reflecting the flow and rhythm of his inner life.

Legend has it that t'ai chi originated with a Taoist monk who observed a magpie trying to attack a snake. With its controlled, writhing, sinuous movements, the watchful snake eluded the frantic bird – a triumph of calm control over frenzied agitation.

Many of the movements in t'ai chi represent the liquid flow of water, while circular movements express unity and wholeness.

As with yoga, t'ai chi has been practised for thousands of years, and for many it is a serious lifetime commitment, a discipline of the mind as well as the body. Traditionally, the art was always passed from a master to his students and its mysteries never written down. Although there are now many books available on t'ai chi, the best way to learn remains to find a teacher. Classes are now widely available throughout the UK, and there is likely to be one near you.

The Alexander Technique

Frederick Alexander (1869–1955) was an Australian reciter or actor whose career was overshadowed by a tendency to lose his voice and become hoarse. Alexander consulted many doctors and tried many conventional remedies in order to correct this distressing – and career-ruining – tendency, all to no avail. Eventually he decided to observe himself and see if by simply watching himself (in mirrors) he could discover what he was doing that was causing his voice to dry up. This period of intense self-study lasted a decade and what he discovered formed the basis of the Alexander Technique. In 1904 Alexander took his technique to London where he became something of a celebrity, as actors and performers flocked to learn from him.

Today, a high proportion of actors, dancers and other stage performers practice the Alexander Technique on a daily basis, and many academies of drama and music include AT lessons on the curriculum. When an actor stands and moves in a balanced way, not tensing his throat and neck, he can produce and project his voice better. A musician such as a violinist who sits well, with a minimum of effort, will play better.

Simply put, the Alexander Technique is about

posture and co-ordination. (It is not, however, quite that simple!) One of Alexander's books is called The Use of the Self, and that provides a clue to the underlying philosophy of the technique. We can use our bodies as a musician uses an instrument but we seldom do: for most of us, our bodies are somewhat rusty machines that hold tension which in turns leads to 'stress blockages' in the neck and the back. What the technique teaches is economy of effort, and a more fluid, co-ordinated, balanced 'use of the self'.

One of Alexander's main passions in life was horses, and it's easy to see why. He loved their perfect balance, their apparently effortless movement, their grace, their suppleness. We all had these qualities as children –an Alexander teacher will usually suggest that you look at a child, and observe the way in which they naturally balance their heads on their bodies – but we have lost them as we grow and adopt unnatural poses for long hours (such as hunched over a school desk, or flopped in front of the TV) and as our bodies absorb tension from the world around us.

Have you ever sat on a bus, and watched people in the street walking past you? Or on a train in a station, and watched people moving up and down the platform? It is sad and shocking to see how many people grimace with the effort of moving, as if their very existence is making them tense up and hold themselves in. The human body holds memory just as the brain does. Your brain remembers events and incidents and people, but the tissues of the body 'remember' stress and tension. When you see adults with their legs and arms crossed in a highly defensive posture, it is as if they are literally holding their tension to themselves in case it falls out.

Frederick Alexander himself believed that his Technique could only be taught on a one-to-one basis, and for many years this was the only way in which it was passed on. And as many of Alexander's clients were actors and artists and wealthy people, the technique itself became a rather exclusive commodity.

This has begun to change, and more and more teachers try to hold classes and reach a wider circle of people. Day or weekend workshops are also more frequent. Classes are good, but it is true that if you can afford it the best start of all is to have a short course of sessions on a one-to-one basis with a trained Alexander teacher. These will cost between £10–£30 for a session (these last between 40 minutes–one hour) depending on the area in which you live and the experience of your teacher, but they are well worth it.

In these sessions, the client lies – fully clothed, but wearing loose and unrestrictive garments – either on the floor or on a treatment bed, while the teacher gently and slowly manipulates each limb and the spine to achieve maximum rest and extension. With the pull of gravity and our own inner tensions, the spine tends to shrink. Many people have found that they are taller after an Alexander session – this is actually true, as the release of tension allows the spine to 'let go' and the body simply extends to the true height it was meant to be.

A cornerstone of the technique is the 'Semi-Supine Position'. Almost every individual session or class will spend approximately 20 minutes lying in this restful position, during which the vertebrae (normally squashed by gravity as we stand and move) can fully release and open like a flower.

Try this for yourself. You need to be alone, in a quiet room, dressed in loose and comfortable clothes. Remove your shoes. You will also need approximately two or three paperback books as a rest for your head. To gauge how many books you need (a teacher will be able to tell you exactly) stand against a wall with your bottom and shoulder blades touching the wall. Stand as normally as you can, as if the wall was not there. Now use your fingers to measure the space between the back of your head and the wall. Add one inch to this, and this measurement should correspond to the thickness of the books you need to lie on.

1. Place the books on the floor, where you head is going to be. Stand a few feet away from the books with your back to them – roughly where your feet will be when you lie down – in a relaxed position. Be aware of any tension in your neck or your back, and try to release it by breathing deeply and slowly. Unclench your hands and be aware of them falling loosely by your sides.

2. Drop on to your right knee, and then on your left, and then sit on your knees, and then move on to your bottom with your feet drawn up close to your bottom. Do every movement slowly and with as little effort as possible.

3. Now put your hands behind you, check where the books are, and ease yourself down.

4. Your head is resting on the paperback books, your knees are hip-width apart and drawn up (but not too close to the body – about a foot from your bottom). Your hands should rest gently on your tummy, with your elbows out to the side. Your position is not unlike that of a woman about to give birth. You should be comfortable enough to remain in this

position for 20 minutes.

In a class or an individual session, the teacher will use this 20 minutes to take you through a visualisation exercise in which each part of the fact is focused on in turn and you are invited to give attention to that part of the body – not to tense it, not to do anything with it, just bring the focus of your mind on to it for a moment. Imagine your back opening like a sunflower, and the feeling of warmth and wellbeing as each muscle unfolds, relaxes, and lengthens.

Alone at home and lying in this position, you can do a number of things. It's recommended that you don't close your eyes: the aim is not to fall asleep, but to be alert and conscious of the body. Breathe deeply at all times. Some people like to listen to relaxation tapes; there is a tape available which talks you through the semi-supine position (details in the Glen Park book described below). I have heard of people with a specific medical condition who spend the 20 minutes focusing on the part of the body with that condition, visualising it and stroking it.

Whatever you choose to do or not, this is your time. A time for you to spend with your body, enjoying it, resting it, cherishing it. Don't do, be.

In getting up from the semi-supine position,

remember to do so slowly and gently. Take as long as you need. You've just spent 20 minutes unfolding yourself, so you don't want to clench it and tense it again at once. The best way is to roll over on to one side, and then gradually get on to all fours. From all fours move back to a squat-kneeling position, then kneel upright. Then lift one leg in front of you, place that foot on the ground, and use that to push yourself upright. Try to make every movement soft, without jarring or forcing your body at any stage.

Further reading
F. M. Alexander, *The Use of the Self*. Gollancz.
Michael Gelb, *Body Learning*. Aurum Press.
Glen Park, *The Art of Changing*. Ashgrove.

Osteopathy and chiropractic

Tension and stress endured over long periods of time lead, almost inevitably, to back and neck problems. The best solution is to relieve the stress and correct your posture so that these problems do not occur, but when they do, more and more people are find help by visiting either an osteopath or a chiropractor.

Osteopathy is a therapy in which the combination of massage (to ensure efficient circulation and ease muscular tension) and manipulation (of the skeleton) aims to return the whole body to a state of correct balance. Osteopathy is a holistic therapy, so the osteopath will want to know about your eating and lifestyle habits, and your postural habits at work and while relaxing. With the advent of PCs and the fact that many people spend long hours working in front of a computer, osteopaths can give helpful advice about correct ways of sitting and working to minimise discomfort and damage.

With the implementation of the Registration of Osteopaths Act in 1993, all osteopaths must be registered practitioners who have followed a specific course of training and the profession is regulated by the General Osteopathic Council.

Chiropractic will soon be similarly registered

and works on many of the same principles as osteopathy. If you go to see a chiropractor, expect vigorous massage and manipulation with the intention of re-aligning the spine so that pressure on nerves (leading to pain) is relieved.

USEFUL ADDRESSES

Acupuncture
British Acupuncture Council
Park House
206–208 Latimer Road
London W10 6RE
Tel: 0208 735 0400

Alcohol problems
Alcoholics Anonymous
P O Box 1, Stonebow House
Stonebow,
York Y01 7NJ
Tel: 01904 644026

Alexander Technique
Society of Teachers of the Alexander Technique
20 London House
266 Fulham Road
London SW10 9EL
Tel: 0207 351 0828

Aromatherapy
Aromatherapy Organisations Council
P O Box 355
Croydon CR9 2QP
Tel: 020 8251 7912

Bach Flower Therapy
The Dr Edward Bach Centre
Mount Vernon
Sotwell, Wallingford
Oxon OX10 0PZ
Tel: 01491 834678

Chiropractic
The British Chiropractic Association
Blagrave House
Blagrave Street, Reading
Berks RG1 1QB
Tel: 0118 950 5950

Debt Management
Alexander Rose Debt Management Ltd
The Dovecote
Castle Bromwich Hall, Chester Road
Castle Bromwich, Birmingham B36 9DE
Tel: 07000 273583

Homeopathy
British Homeopathic Association
27a Devonshire Street
London W1N 1RJ
Tel: 020 7935 2163

Homeopathy
Faculty of Homeopathy
15 Clerkenwell Close
London EC1R 0AA
Tel: 020 7566 7810

Society of Homeopaths
2 Artizan Road
Northampton NN1 4HU

UK Homeopathic Medical Association
243 The Broadway
Southall
Middlesex UB1 3AN

The Irish Society of Homeopathics
Ruxton Court
35-37 Dominick Street
Galway
Rep of Ireland
Tel: 091 565040

Osteopathy
General Osteopathic Council
176 Tower Bridge Road
London SE1 3LU
Tel: 020 757 6655

Osteopathy/Naturopathy
The Ford Clinic
316 Howth Road
Dublin 5
Rep of Ireland
Tel: 1491 839489

PMS
National Association for Pre-menstrual Syndrome
Helpline: 01732 760012
Website: www.pms.org.uk

Psychotherapy and counselling
British Association for Counselling
1 Regent Place
Rugby
Warwickshire CV21 2PJ
Tel: 01788 578328
email: bac@BAC.co.uk

Reflexology
Association of Reflexologists
27 Old Gloucester Street
London WC1N 3XX
Tel: 0870 5673320

The Irish Reflexologists Institute
Blenheim Cross
Dunmore Road,
Waterford
Republic of Ireland
Tel: 051 875444

Scottish School of Reflexology
P O Box 1
Ayr
Tel: 01292 287142

Shiatsu
The Shiatsu Society
Suite D, Barber House
Storeys Bar Road
Fengate
Peterborough PE1 5YS
Tel: 01733 758341

Shiatsu Society of Ireland
Belgrove, Sandyford Village
Dublin 18
Republic of Ireland

Yoga
British Wheel of Yoga
1 Hamilton Place
Boston Road
Sleaford
Lincs NG34 7ES
Tel: 01529 303233

Scottish Yoga Teachers Association
Frances Corr
26 Buckingham Terrace
Edinburgh EH4 3AE
Tel: 0131 343 3553

Yoga Therapy Centre
Royal London Homeopathic Hospital
60 Great Ormond Street
London WC1N 3HR
Tel: 020 7419 7195